UNSPE

The Hidden Truth Behind
The World's Fastest Growing Crime

Raymond Bechard

Compel Publishing
New York
A Division of Compel Communications, LLC
www.CompelCommunications.com

Published in New York, New York by Compel Publishing,
a division of Compel Communications, LLC.

Published in association with Ahava Kids.
Ahava Kids, a 501(c)3 tax exempt corporation, in Old Saybrook, CT,
is completely responsible for the content of this material.
All proceeds from this book benefit Ahava Kids.
www.AhavaKids.org

ISBN 0-4937-4585-2

Printed in the United States of America
First edition, November 2006

For little Karen.

She looked at me with *hope*.

Acknowledgements

My deep thanks to those who helped me fight this battle.

Every individual supporter of Ahava Kids.
Donna Hart for her tireless editing and exquisite design work, and for hope.
Glenn Morelli and Lisa Mazzotta for their endless support and encouragement.
Bob Carr for his excellent publishing and production advice, and for his friendship.
The people of The First Cathedral for their faith.
James Jensen for his faith in the mission.
Patty Swanson for her photography and assistance.
Ben Martin for the cover layout.
Jon Rondeau and Jammie Welch of New Wave Industries for their talent and patience.
Mary Macey for proofreading everything.
Frances Ann Janosco for her kindness and expediency.
Richard and Bonnie Schuman for a safe haven.
My Mother for knowing the book was already done.
My Father for expecting this all along.

Introduction

Maybe you shouldn't read this book.

It is certainly not for everyone. What you will discover here is difficult, often devastating. It is the written equivalent of exposing yourself to the images in movies like *Saving Private Ryan*, *Schindler's List* or *The Passion of the Christ.*

Certainly, I am not saying that my attempt to convey the world of *child trafficking* through this book achieves the quality or significance of these great and important films. I only cite them because of the raw style by which they expose the viewer to profound historical incidents. In order to truly impart the horrible experience of the Normandy invasion, the Holocaust or the Crucifixion, these films ruthlessly carried their audiences through crushing images of horror. That was their purpose and intent.

So it is with this book.

Make no mistake, there are horrors here. I do not make this warning to be dramatic. That is not necessary. I mention this only to prepare you, the reader, for what is to come. These are not things you can discuss in detail at a pleasant dinner party, a family picnic or at the office. The facts, images, and stories herein are meant to inform the reader of crimes that are occurring continually, with unimagined multiplicity, all over the world at this very moment. While this book does not have the advantage of presenting its message with the talent and drama of the films previously cited, it does have the immediacy of a real and undeniable global crisis.

The one urgent fact that may motivate you to continue is this: *while you are holding this book, thousands of children are being sold into slavery.* They will be used for child soldiers, forced labor and even body parts. But, the vast majority will be used for sex.

* * *

A good friend of mine is a collector of antiquities pertaining to the African-American experience. I was attending an exhibit of his fascinating collection when he approached me holding a very heavy object.

I wanted to say hello to him, but the dark metal item in his hands stole my attention. Without bothering to greet me, he quietly said, "Here, take this for a minute."

I lifted the thing from his hands and immediately felt the weight; about twenty pounds. Only a quick glance told me what it was. Yet, the longer I looked at it the heavier it became. Obviously very old and forged by hand, it consisted of a thick metal ring with a diameter of about six inches. Attached to the ring was a length of unbreakable, rusted chain.

"Is this what I think it is?" I asked him.

"Yes," he said. "They put it around their necks."

I was holding the chains of a slave, an American slave, from the early nineteenth century. This was far more than a relic. In my hands was the very thing that held one person in the complete possession and control of another with absolutely no freedom, liberty or escape.

I could not shake the awful dread of knowing the pain it had brought upon men, women and children, all long dead. Today, years after the experience of holding those chains, I can still feel their evil weight in my hands. It is not an easy weight to carry.

In the same way my friend came to me, holding something that would change the way I look at the world and my place in it, I now come to you with this book and say, "Here, take this for a minute."

While not made of heavy steel, the stories you find here are just as powerful.

The stories of child trafficking throughout this book are told by the children themselves; children who have been rescued and are now protected and cared for. Having been saved and interviewed by people of inspiring courage and dedication, they can safely tell their stories to all of us.

We must listen to what they are telling us because they speak for those who remain enslaved; those whose voices we cannot hear. *This book is their voice.* They are still living the nightmare and the tragedy of their young lives is yet unspoken.

For that reason, I truly hope you will look beyond the horrible truth herein, beyond the *unspeakable.*

One

"On this trip, I've had sex with a fourteen-year-old girl in Mexico and a fifteen-year-old in Colombia. I'm helping them financially. If they don't have sex with me, they may not have enough food. If someone has a problem with me doing this, let UNICEF feed them."

Retired U.S. Schoolteacher
Source: U.S. Department of Justice

I am Tanya*

Victims of a Special Evil

* * *

"My friend organized for me to get a job in Egypt. We traveled together from Chisinau to Moscow where I got a plane to Egypt. When I got to the airport in Egypt, I was paired with a man in order to walk through customs and immigration. People were waiting for me and they took me to a five-star hotel. I gave up my passport at the reception of the hotel and never saw it again. They put me in a car and we drove for a really long time. We went to a place where Bedouins are and those Bedouins took us through the desert. At one point, I heard gunshots and I think a girl was killed. They kill you or beat you if they don't like your attitude. We had to walk for hours and hours through the desert where there were landmines. They pointed out the mines to us in the sand. We hardly ate and I lost 10 kilos by the time I got to Israel. When we got out of the desert, we were taken to a town in Israel, where the Bedouins arranged for us to be sold. Many girls were traveling with me, and all the girls going to Israel go through the same route and the same situation."

Tanya, 14
Source: UNICEF

* * *

* All children's names have been changed to protect their identities. Names and titles of authorities, scholars, and officials have not been changed unless otherwise noted.

Tanya's journey is not unique. In fact, as told to the people who rescued her, Tanya's story of deception, coercion, and abuse is common in the world today and throughout history. Tanya became a slave to organized crime's fastest growing enterprise: *Child trafficking.*

* * *

Child trafficking is not a new crime, only more organized and widespread. The possession and abuse of children has existed for thousands of years. The drastic difference now is that the crime of trafficking children is far more efficient and profitable. Today, child trafficking is an expanding and lucrative global industry. After drug dealing, "trafficking of humans is tied with arms dealing as the second largest criminal industry in the world, and is the fastest growing," according to the U.S. Department of Health & Human Services.

The reasons are simple, as worldwide organized crime increases the number of children it controls and makes available, the number of its customers increase. As customers increase, so does the demand for more. To meet the growing demand, the illegal market for exploited young people expands uncontrollably. It is an economic cycle fueled by the torture of children.

Against their will, children are trafficked mostly into the international sex trade for prostitution, sex tourism, and pornography. Outside of sexual exploitation children are used for organ harvesting, forced labor, soldiers in rebel armies, domestic servitude, street beggars and camel jockeys.

Whatever their purpose, whatever act they are forced to perform, the victims of child trafficking become, by any definition, slaves. Yet, the enslavement of children is not new. However, the rate at which children are trapped in this downward spiral to death is increasing to unprecedented levels.

According to the most reliable sources at the United Nations, the U.S. Department of State, and the International Labor Organization among others, human trafficking is the third largest criminal industry for global organized crime.

Conservatively, the United Nations estimates that at least 1.2 million children were transported for the purposes of exploitation in 2005. These estimates have increased each year since records have been kept. Following narcotics and weapons, the trafficking of human beings brings in annual worldwide profits ranging from 7 to 13 billion dollars.

The advantages to buying and selling humans, especially children, are many:

- *Unlike other trafficked goods, it is not illegal or suspicious to have a child in your presence*, making it a high profit and relatively low risk commodity.
- *Demand is growing* as organized crime becomes more sophisticated in the ways in which it provides children for exploitation, customers can easily and safely gain access.
- *One child can be sold multiple times.* Unlike other illegal commodities, some children are forced to service customers 20 to 30 times a day.

* * *

"Maria is prostituted by her aunt. Maria is obliged to sell her body exclusively to foreign tourists in Costa Rica; she only works mornings as she has to attend school in the afternoon. Maria is in the fifth grade."

Source: Report on Human Trafficking
U.S. Department of State

* * *

"Over the last 10 years, the number of women and children [who] have been trafficked has multiplied so that they are now on par with estimates of the numbers of Africans who were enslaved in the 16th and 17th centuries," says Dr. Laura Lederer, who has been studying the issue of sexual trafficking for 20 years at Harvard University.

Lederer is one of many voices around the world attempting to bring the topic of child trafficking to the forefront of public discussion, awareness and action. Among those voices is the United States Department of State, which has issued extensive reports focusing on human trafficking since 2000. Religious organizations and private foundations are also beginning to rally around these forgotten children.

Whether the information and subsequent calls for justice are coming from individuals, governments, religious organizations, or private groups, their conclusions are all very similar.

Child trafficking is a human rights violation. Fundamentally, child trafficking, like all forms of slavery, violates the universal human right to life, liberty, and freedom from slavery in all its forms.

Trafficking of children steals the need every child has to grow up in a safe environment and the right to be free from sexual abuse and exploitation.

Trafficked children suffer irreparable damage to their physical and mental health. The severe risks to which they are exposed often lead to early pregnancy, forced drug addiction, AIDS and other sexually transmitted diseases, and ultimately death.

Children victimized by trafficking are often inadequately protected by the law and may be treated as criminals. In some countries, there is no protection for victims brave enough to assist in the prosecution of traffickers.

Victims in these situations do not know how to escape the violence or where to go for help.

If they survive and escape from their captors each child needs extensive therapy, health monitoring and recovery.

* * *

Most trafficking of children begins by gaining possession of them either by kidnapping, coercion, or simply purchasing them. Then, through a hidden and complex route of people and bribes, the children are moved to other countries or, depending on their purpose and location, to another area of their own country. Finally, at the destination, the child is typically made to provide whatever services their new owner forces upon them.

To enforce whatever acts the child is continually made to do, there are certain elements of control common to all trafficking situations. Through efficient and well developed skills of manipulation, traffickers use threats, intimidation, assault, rape, drugs, violence and any other methods they find useful in obtaining the highest level of profitability from the child.

Wherever the victims end up, they are always at a severe disadvantage. Imagine Tanya, isolated and unable to speak the language; completely unfamiliar with the culture in which she is trapped. She does not have immigration documents or any legal status or rights. Most important, she has lost the love and support of family and friends. She is completely alone, making her even more vulnerable to the demands and threats of those who control her every move.

Every moment of every day she will be exposed to humiliation, uncontrollable violence, disease, rape, and other sexual abuse that she cannot begin to understand.

At first terror keeps her from running away. She is afraid of the people who keep her locked up, the customers who abuse her, the authorities, the police, everyone. Later, as her mind begins to shut down from the constant torture and fear, physical pain becomes normal. She no longer cares about staying alive because she has expected death for so long.

A child with no will to live can no longer be controlled by fear alone. She is given drugs until she is addicted. It doesn't take long. Now, the only thing she cares about is getting her drug. And she will do anything to get it.

* * *

"Each year, . . . human beings are bought, sold or forced across the world's borders. Among them are hundreds of thousands of teenage girls, and others as young as five, who fall victim to the sex trade. This commerce in human life generates billions of dollars each year, much of which is used to finance organized crime. There's a special evil in the abuse and exploitation of the most innocent and vulnerable. The victims of the sex trade see little of life before they see the very worst of life, an underground of brutality and lonely fear. Those who create these victims and profit from their suffering must be severely punished. Those who patronize this industry debase themselves and deepen the misery of others. And governments that tolerate this trade are tolerating a form of slavery."

President George W. Bush

* * *

Child trafficking is not something people generally discuss. It's far too repulsive. In their disgust, they turn the topic of conversation to anything else but the matter at hand. Or, they attempt to simplify their view of it by relating what they know to a movie they saw about trafficking, perhaps an afternoon talk show, or a television news program that focused on it one night long ago.

Either way, in just a few moments the topic is gone. The very subject of children being bought and sold for the pleasure of adults is *unspeakable*. It cannot be described without offending the senses. It cannot be visualized without harming the spirit. It cannot be ignored without damaging the soul.

Until now, we have protected ourselves by leaving it unspoken.

Yet, if we permit ourselves to finally face the truth, Tanya's story is just one of many that allow us to fully understand the impact and scope of child trafficking. The stories of other children, as told to those who interviewed them after their rescue, lead us down a very dark path. Their words terrify and anger all who dare to travel where they take us.

It is important to remember that as you read what has happened to each of them, they are the lucky ones; the ones blessed enough to have been rescued and fortunate enough to have survived to tell us about it.

The others, perhaps millions of them, are still lost in the darkness, waiting and yes, suffering. They cannot tell their stories to anyone because they cannot speak. They remain imprisoned in a nightmare known only to them. Enslavement has taken away their voices, no matter how loud they scream.

They are children, held captive, and whatever they may want to tell us, their words are silent, unspoken, *unspeakable*.

* * *

Two

I am Nhoi

The Evolution of Slaves

* * *

Nhoi came from a poor community in rural Thailand. At 15, seeking to escape rape and sexual abuse in her foster family, she found a foreign labor agent in Bangkok who advertised well-paid waitress jobs in Japan. She flew to Japan and later learned that she had entered Japan on a tourist visa under a false identity. On her arrival in Japan, she was taken to a karaoke bar where the owner raped her, subjected her to a blood test and then bought her. "I felt like a piece of flesh being inspected," she recounted. The brothel madam told Nhoi that she had to pay off a debt of over 10,000 U.S. Dollars to repay her travel expenses. She was warned that girls who tried to escape were brought back by the Japanese mafia, severely beaten, and their debts doubled. The only way to pay off the debt was to see as many clients as quickly as possible. Some clients beat the girls with sticks, belts and chains until they bled. If the victims returned crying, they were beaten by the madam and told that they must have provoked the client. The prostitutes routinely used drugs before sex "so that we didn't feel so much pain." Most clients refused to use condoms. The victims were given pills to avoid pregnancy and pregnancies were terminated with home abortions. Victims who managed to pay off their debt and work independently were often arrested by the police, fined, imprisoned, and raped before being deported.

Source: U.S. State Department

* * *

For most of us, *slavery* is merely a historic concept. The very word *slavery* instantly brings to mind the transatlantic slave trade which brought Africans to the Americas or Jewish slavery under Pharaoh in the days of Moses. It is easy for us to believe that thousands of years after Moses led his people out of Egypt, the United States of America ended slavery at the close of the Civil War.

From our early education, we are taught that the abolition of slavery in the late 1800s was completely successful. After centuries of this shameful blight, the enslavement of people, buying and selling individuals, shipping them from their homes to far off lands and lifetimes of forced labor and oppression, was no longer an issue.

Even if we know nothing about the slave trade, it is something we consider as part of our past rather than our present.

The reality of our world today is quite different from what we believe.

The truth is *slavery never ended.* It never came close to ending. In fact, there are more enslaved people in the world today than in any point in history.

In the early years of the 21st century millions of men, women and children around the world are forced to live as slaves. Although this exploitation is not called slavery, the conditions are the same. People are sold like objects, forced to work for little or no pay and are at the mercy of others who control them with absolute authority.

Despite the fact that it is banned in most of the countries where it is practiced, slavery is illegal and very rarely sanctioned by any recognized government in the world, the enslavement of individuals is more prevalent than ever before.

While important, there is only a semantic difference between *slavery* and *enslavement.* In the modern world, no legitimate governments have laws providing for *legal human ownership.* This is the old model of *slavery.*

The demand for slavery, however, still exists. As it is with the demand for illegal drugs or weaponry, the criminal factor takes over when the law bans anything the market wants. And right now the global marketplace wants human beings. To meet this demand and to reap its profits, the outlawed practice of legal slavery has been replaced by coercion, fraud, and violent force. This is *enslavement.*

There are also historic differences. Along with a basis in legal ownership, traditional *slavery* was also based on divisions along ethnic and racial lines. Typically, slaves were expensive and the relationships between slaves and their owners were often long-term, sometimes lasting for generations. Within the framework of modern *enslavement* slaves are inexpensive, even disposable. The vast majority are poor, vulnerable, and dispossessed rather than from particular racial or ethnic groups.

In any case, *the person is a slave*. The difference in definitions of these terms means nothing to the person who is owned, controlled, and imprisoned forever within the walls of a hidden world.

It is important to note that there are common characteristics which distinguish slavery from other human rights violations. A slave is someone who is:

- forced to work or perform any act through mental or physical threat;
- owned or controlled by another human being, usually through mental or physical abuse;
- treated as a commodity or bought and sold as property;
- physically constrained or has restrictions placed on his/her freedom of movement.

* * *

As the world became fully aware of the atrocities committed by Nazi Germany during World War II, there was an unprecedented consensus throughout the global community that the newly formed charter of the United Nations did not sufficiently clarify the human rights it was established to protect. In response, the General Assembly of the United Nations adopted and proclaimed the *Universal Declaration of Human Rights* on December 10, 1948. The Declaration outlined the organization's view on the human rights which are guaranteed to all people and was referred to by Eleanor Roosevelt as "a Magna Carta for all mankind."

A strong statement, it is simply a list of clear objectives to be followed by governments and is not in any way a part of international law nor is it legally binding. It is, however, a powerful tool in applying diplomatic and moral pressure to governments that violate any of its articles.

The 1968 United Nations International Conference on Human Rights decided it "constitutes an obligation for the members of the international community" to all persons. The declaration has served as the foundation for the original two legally binding UN human rights covenants, the International Covenant on Civil and Political Rights, and the International Covenant on Economic, Social and Cultural Rights.

The Declaration contains thirty articles outlining individual human rights. Generally, the most important of these are considered to be:

- The right to life, liberty, property and security of person.
- The right to an education.
- The right to employment, paid holidays, protection against unemployment, and social security.
- The right to participate fully in cultural life.
- Freedom from torture or cruel, inhumane treatment or punishment.
- Freedom of thought, conscience and religion.
- Freedom of expression and opinion.

Along with this Declaration, the 1956 *UN Supplementary Convention on the Abolition of Slavery, the Slave Trade and Institutions and Practices Similar to Slavery,* the nations of the world wanted no person to be a slave anywhere.

It didn't work. More than half a century after the United Nations' first declaration to end slavery, women from Eastern Europe are forced into prostitution, children are trafficked between West African countries and men are bonded to work as slaves on Brazilian agricultural estates. Contemporary slavery has taken on several forms and affects people of all ages, sex and race everywhere in the world.

Among the fastest growing forms of modern day human bondage, "*Sex slavery* is the largest category of trans-national slavery," says John Miller, former Director of the Office to Monitor and Combat Trafficking In Persons for the U.S. Department of State. Replacing the legal and systematic slave trade which existed for millennia throughout the world, the industry is now under the control of organized crime rings, gangsters, pimps, corrupt government officials and law enforcement ranks, creating a situation where "more than half of human slavery involves the selling of women, girls, and boys to commercial sex traffickers. Each year, two million women and children worldwide are forced into brutal sex with strangers," says Miller.

In Thailand, young women and children are forced to work as slave prostitutes, who work only to pay off thousands of dollars of debts imposed by their organized traffickers. Forced also to pay exorbitant monthly expenses, they can be made to perform 4,000 sexual acts a year to meet their quota, $10 at a time, according to Kevin Bales, Director of Free the Slaves, an organization that works to end slavery worldwide. Once trapped in these situations, it is nearly impossible for a girl to escape, no matter how much money she makes. Bales met "one woman working as a sex slave in a brothel in Thailand who was purchased for $2,000 and had made approximately $80,000 for them. After two or three years, if they are not sick or dying of AIDS, they might be freed if their quota has been met. However, long before they reach that point they are no longer profitable. Customers don't want them anymore."

A three-year study by the U.N. on violence against women stated there is a "gendercide of 200 million women missing" in the world today, some of which can be traced to 700,000 women sold into prostitution worldwide annually. According to UNICEF statistics, the sex trafficking industry's exploitation of children alone earns them $12 billion a year.

Several international organizations, including the International Organization for Migration (IOM) have shown these numbers to be much higher. This is because so many victims are still trapped and unable to seek help or, if they are able to, file reports with law enforcement "as they do not see themselves as victims, fear reprisals against themselves or their families, fear being judged for what has happened to them, or are afraid the authorities will treat them as criminals rather than victims," states Mónica Peruffo, with the IOM anti-trafficking in persons program in Colombia.

* * *

While the brutal experience of all slaves throughout history has many similarities, the slaves of today have much more than their freedom taken away. Often they are betrayed by their families, ignored by their communities, forcefully addicted to drugs and treated as criminals by law enforcement wherever they go. To survive, they cannot show themselves or admit who they really are. They are robbed of their identity. They cease to be who they were or, in the case of children, who they could have been.

Occasionally, someone makes a movie featuring a storyline where slavery never ended. Movies like *C.S.A. The Confederate States of America* which explores what life would be like if the South had won the Civil War, or *Manderlay,* which takes place in 1933 at a plantation that still uses slave labor, use fictional "what if" scenarios to examine contemporary society's racial climate and relations.

Reality never fails to be stranger and more horrifying than any fiction Hollywood can create. "What if slavery never ended?" is itself fiction. Saying that slavery has ended is like turning your back on your neighbor's burning house and declaring the fire out. Yet, we accept the end of historic slavery, glad that its long chapter is gone from the human experience. Turning away from modern enslavement, we righteously proclaim, "Never Again!"

The truth is being ignored. It is happening again. And it is happening now more than every before.

* * *

Three

I am Talia

Slavery Comes of Age

* * *

Talia was approached by an acquaintance who told her about restaurants in the United States in need of workers. Hoping to make enough money to support her daughter and parents, Talia accepted the offer and was brought from Mexico to Texas. When she arrived, however, she found that there was no restaurant job. The boss expected her to work as a prostitute to pay off her smuggling debt. When she resisted, she was beaten. If she or the other women with her refused a customer, they were raped. She was 18 years old, with no money and no way to get home. Talia found herself constantly under guard. She and the other women were transported to different locations every few weeks, so they never knew where they were. The armed guards also threatened to injure their family members in Mexico if the women tried to escape. "I did not come to the United States to be a prostitute. I came to find a better future for my family. No woman or child would want to be a sex slave and endure the evil that I have gone through."

Source: International Organization for Migration

* * *

Human trafficking,* which includes child trafficking, is modern-day slavery. Defined by the United Nations as "the illegal trade and exploitation of people forced into labor through coercion, fraud, sale, threat, or deception," human trafficking is today the largest and most widely practiced form of slavery in history. It is also the third largest and fastest growing criminal industry in the world.

Not limited to the possession of one human being by another, it also includes human rights abuses such as debt bondage, deprivation of liberty, and lack of control over one's own freedom.

Further, human trafficking does not necessarily involve the movement of victims across an international borders or any distance at all.

Human trafficking is more complex than the slavery of old as it involves coercion and smuggling leaving slavery as the final step. Typically, human trafficking is characterized by three stages:

1. ***Recruitment*** of trafficking victims takes place primarily in developing countries like Asia, Eastern Europe, the former Soviet Union, Latin America and Africa. Countries of origin are generally marked by economic and political instability.
2. ***Transportation*** typically involves a complex travel route and paid handlers. Depending on the length of transit and the economic situation at the destination, traffickers often make enormous profits for transportation and delivery.
3. ***Exploitation***. Wherever their destination may be, trafficking victims are usually exploited by their recruiters for financial profit, and are sold or leased to others. The traffickers usually hold their victims under conditions of physical captivity, using force, threats, indentured servitude, drugs, and violence to motivate them to perform whatever service is required.

* * *

* The distinction of human trafficking from child trafficking is made here simply because people of all ages, not just children, are being sold into slavery and abuse across the world.

Under the *Victims of Trafficking and Violence Protection* Act of 2000 (TVPA), the United States Congress defined and criminalized human trafficking more specifically than the UN. The act is extensive and, with proper enforcement, effective.

Among its definitions the TVPA labels "sex trafficking" as one of the "severe forms of trafficking in persons," calling it "a commercial sex act induced by force, fraud, or coercion, or in which the person induced to perform such act has not attained 18 years of age; or the recruitment, harboring, transportation, provision, or obtaining of a person for labor or services, through the use of force, fraud, or coercion for the purpose of subjection to involuntary servitude, peonage, debt bondage, or slavery."

The TVPA goes on to define those guilty of "forced labor" anyone who, "knowingly provides or obtains the labor or services of a person by threats of serious harm to, or physical restraint against, that person or another person; by means of any scheme, plan, or pattern intended to cause the person to believe that, if the person did not perform such labor or services, that person or another person would suffer serious harm or physical restraint; or by means of the abuse or threatened abuse of law or the legal process."

* * *

Human trafficking is often confused or interchanged with human smuggling. While they are similar, the two are distinct criminal offenses. Under U.S. Code, "human smuggling" is defined as "knowingly [having] encouraged, induced, assisted, abetted or aided any other alien to enter or try to enter the United States." This may sound exactly like "trafficking," but there are several major differences and objectives to each crime. The major difference is that smuggling inherently involves people who want to be moved from one place to another or across borders.

When a boat is captured with several people from Asian hidden deep within its hold, trying to make their way illegally into the United States, this is smuggling. The people on that boat, no matter how filthy and dangerous the conditions of their transportation, want to be brought to a specific destination and have paid someone for the service. The same is true for people being transported in the back of a sweltering truck across the Mexican border into the U.S. They are willing participants. Again, smuggling.

Trafficking occurs when the person being relocated has no choice in the matter. Someone has taken possession of them or has them within their control. They are being taken without their consent or, especially in the case of young people, understanding.

Another major difference is that a smuggled person can choose to leave at any point during the process and is free to go once they have been taken to their destination. Not true for those who are trafficked. They are completely controlled by those who are moving them and those who take possession of them at their final destination. They cannot leave. They have no free will. Trafficked persons are slaves.

The *smuggled* person, while participating willingly in an illegal act, is free. The *trafficked* person makes no willing participation and has no freedom.

There is a storyline in the Academy Award-winning movie *Crash* in which an old van full of hidden, *smuggled* Asians inadvertently falls into the hands of Lucien, a very shady operator of an automobile chop shop. The thief who stole the van, Anthony, does not know there are people chained in its windowless cargo section; he is just trying to get the best price for the stolen vehicle. Thinking he is only buying a battered, stolen van, Lucien discovers the frightened human cargo locked inside. Looking through the back door he smiles, instantly calculating the value of this enormous profit now trapped in his garage. “I’ll give you $500 a piece and you can keep the van,” he tells Anthony. This is a windfall and his motive is clear. He will use these people for whatever purpose he wants.

Wanting and willing only to be *smuggled* into the United States, the stowaways are now at the mercy of this one man who will take possession of them and their destiny against their will. In just minutes they will become victims of *trafficking*.

Later, in one of the movie’s ironically heroic scenes, Anthony is driving the same van along Hollywood Boulevard. Knowing Lucien’s intentions, he didn’t sell the van or its human cargo. Instead, he parks on the side of the road, opens the back door and sets the people free, handing one of them $40 for food. They walk away, bewildered. Welcome to America.

The scene illustrates how closely related smuggling is to trafficking, and how easily one can become the other, especially when criminal elements are controlling the entire process.

The similarities of the process do not end with the treatment of the person being moved. In practice, most of the travel routes and cities used by organized crime throughout the world are the same.

In the United States for example, crossing the border was very easy until the middle 1990s. Prior to that time people entering the U.S. did not need professional smugglers, just small time guides who charged a few dollars to show them the way. Then, as illegal border crossings became a major issue, federal authorities began enforcing the border with increasing efficiency. Even though we hear of "broken borders" today, the problem of illegal immigration across the southern borders of the U.S. was much worse in the past.

With the increased difficulty of illegally entering the country, hardened criminals took on the business of smuggling humans as it became more lucrative. Using very sophisticated surveillance and communications equipment that allows what a Library of Congress report on Criminal and Terrorist Activity in Mexico calls a "technological arms race" with the Border Patrol, smuggling fees have jumped into the thousands of dollars in just a few years.

In 2006 the typical immigrant pays $1,200 to $2,500 to be brought across the border, transported to stopover cities like San Diego, Houston or Phoenix, then shipped to a final destination somewhere in the United States.

The same is true for countries in Eastern Europe and throughout Asia. Organized crime is increasing its operations as authorities crack down on the illegal movement of people. As laws and enforcement get tougher, prices to move and operate illegally increase.

Consequently, the small-time smugglers of the past have been eliminated by the professionals; killed and buried in the deserts of Mexico, the abandoned industrial parks of Moldova and the garbage dumps of Bangkok.

The entire scheme is still fresh within organized crime's stable of operations. There will be extraordinary levels of increasing violence as the top operators ruthlessly come to power and stabilize their hidden industry.

With the entrance of sophisticated organized crime operations onto the stage of human smuggling, there is an inherent danger to those choosing to be smuggled. Once they are in the hands of the professional smugglers, there is nothing to keep them from being held captive for any length of time and for any purpose.

If you are the Smuggler/Trafficker consider your advantages:

You have total control of the people you are smuggling. Whether you have them locked in the back of a truck, the hold of a ship or in the basement of a building, no one is going to question how you contain them or keep them in control.

You have their money. For being smuggled, they either pay you up front or they are indebted to you. Now you have them *and* their money.

You have their free will. They know what they are doing is illegal so they will do anything to avoid getting caught. They also know that being apprehended by authorities will mean severe punishment for them and their families back home. No matter what happens to them or what you do to them, they will keep quiet.

You have taken total control of them, their money and their free will.

Now, the real betrayal begins. With their money in hand you turn around and make a deal with another member of your crime "family," the ones who know how to make the most money from the forced labor of men, women and, most profitable of all, their children. The organization pays you to deliver this group of desperate people wherever they need them.

It's a good day. You've swindled money from the people who paid you to move them and you've been paid by the person to whom you sold them. No one is going to the police. No one is going to tell the next group waiting to be smuggled that you can't be trusted. And no one knows what happens to them once you move them along. Who cares? After all, you have another order to fill.

* * *

While it is true that anyone wishing to be smuggled from one country to the next must pay huge sums of money, most of these people are poor and do not have ready access to that kind of cash. Some will come up with the entire amount in advance by borrowing from loan sharks, family, friends, or anyone willing to give it to them. Of course, they are indebted to these people and must repay the money as quickly as possible. This is actually the safest method of obtaining the necessary funds.

There are other methods for the smuggler to become a trafficker while generating even more profit. This risk comes to others who pay only a deposit or advance on the total amount and must pay the balance to the smugglers in the future. If this is their choice they are faced with years of debt to criminal elements and will most likely face some form of indentured servitude. In order to pay the debt, the new illegal immigrant arrives in the country of destination and usually enters some form of illegal employment or becomes involved in criminal activities arranged by the smugglers. Whatever work they are doing, they are no longer in control of their own destiny. They live in constant peril, completely beholden to those who determine every aspect of their lives.

In any case, they must pay. If they don't, their lives, along with the lives of their families back home, are threatened. They are no longer working for a new life, they are working to simply stay alive. Pay the debt or pay the violent consequences.

Of course, with interest, expenses, and any other charges the smuggler can tack on, the debt never ends. Nor does the slavery in which they find themselves. Worst of all they often travel with their children. And the children are never spared because children are also a source of easy profit.

This is how smuggling directly leads to child trafficking. This is no rare occurrence. It happens every day in every city around the world. The market is growing for children and the suppliers are rushing to meet the demand any way they can.

If an occasional case comes to the light of law enforcement, officials find it difficult to determine whether someone has been smuggled willingly into a country or if they were trafficked by force. However, if both forms of entry result in forced labor of any kind, there is no difference to distinguish; the labor is illegal. Also, if any person under 18 is induced to perform commercial sex acts, it is then always considered trafficking. In either case the safety of the victims and prosecution of the traffickers will only take place if local law enforcement is legitimate and without corruption.

* * *

A husband and wife in the United States convince their relatives in India to allow their daughters to travel to America to receive an education. The husband and wife are the aunt and uncle to the girls. They have promised the girls' parents, who are very poor, that they would provide housing and support for them during their schooling. In order for the girls to receive a student visa, their aunt and uncle enroll them in school in the U.S. The visas are granted and the girls begin their journey to America. Once the girls arrive in the U.S., their aunt and uncle immediately tell them that they will not be attending school. The aunt and uncle never intended to have the girls go to school and only enrolled them for the purpose of fraudulently obtaining the entry visas. At this point, the girls have unwittingly been smuggled into the U.S. using visa fraud. During the next several weeks, the girls are locked in a basement and continually told that if they try to leave, they would be arrested for their involvement in the fraud. Eventually, their uncle takes the girls to local motels where they are made to clean rooms and provide janitorial services. The girls are never paid for their work, all their identification has been taken away, and they are continually reminded that they could be arrested for their involvement in a serious crime. Because the girls are being held against their will through coercion and intimidation and are being forced to work for no pay, they are now victims of trafficking.

Source: U.S. Dept. of State *Trafficking in Persons* Report 2005

* * *

These are just a few of the tremendous risks involved when someone pays to be smuggled into another country. Why take such risks? Leaving home is one matter, but what causes an individual to leave their home, their home*land*, their family, their culture, and everything they value? Typically, there are two major reasons for someone to risk everything, including their children, in order to relocate so drastically.

The first is the *flee* factor. Poverty, unemployment, political oppression, natural disasters, and war cause people to *flee* from their homes every day. Because of circumstances no longer in their control and no matter what the consequences may be to their safety on the road ahead, there is no greater peril than to stay. They are being pushed out against their will and must relocate by all means necessary. This may seem like something that cannot happen in the United States or anywhere in western civilization, but one only needs to recall the thousands desperate to leave New Orleans during and after Hurricane Katrina. Or, in the most extreme case, those who chose to leap rather than face the flames of the World Trade Center.

The worse option is to stay, so they go at any cost. Today and every day across the world, there are hundreds of thousands of people facing this choice.

The second is the *free* factor. From the vantage point of those living in abject poverty, wealthier nations have an enormous, almost mythic draw. Freedom, democracy, employment, and personal safety combine to create a great magnet for humanity. They feel pulled toward a better life and will sacrifice all they know to obtain it.

Whether they relocate to *flee* or be *free*, they are at the mercy of every person they encounter along the way. They make themselves vulnerable to worst part of humanity. And that part of humanity is getting smarter, more ruthless and better organized every day.

* * *

Four

I am Tiola

Children Pay the Highest Price

* * *

Tiola, a young Albanian girl, was thirteen when she started dating twenty-one-year-old Nilin. Charming and attentive, Tiola quickly said "yes" when Nilin asked her to marry him only weeks into their relationship. After a short civil wedding they immediately left for Italy where he claimed to have cousins who could get him a job. Arriving in Italy, Tiola's life changed forever. Nilin locked her in a hotel room and left her. She never saw him again. She remembers what happened next. "A few hours later a group of men entered the room and began to yell at me and beat me. Each one of them took their turn with me. One would hold me down while the others raped me," The leader told Tiola that Dilin had sold her to them for $250. "He said that I had to obey him or else I would be killed." For seven days Tiola was beaten and repeatedly raped. Then, her traffickers sold her a second time to someone whose face she never saw. "He beat my head so badly I could not see out my eyes for two days." She was told if she didn't work as a prostitute, her mother and sister in Albania would be raped and killed. Viola was forced to submit to prostitution until police raided the brothel she was in. She was deported by Italian authorities back to Albania.

Source: UNICEF

* * *

Throughout history *children* have always paid the highest price for war, poverty, disease, ignorance and exploitation.

Child trafficking is not confined to the borders of any one country. It happens in every nation. UNICEF values the global market of child trafficking at over $12 billion a year with over 1.2 million child victims. Yet, wherever it takes place the procedure is similar: A young girl or boy is brought from one place to another by someone who pays the family and promises to educate the child or find them a good job. Instead, years of exploitation and abuse await them.

The trafficking of children, in all its forms, has existed for centuries. As we define it today, adults have long taken and exploited children for whatever purposes their young lives were needed at the time.

The mass migration from Europe to the United States in the late 1800s brought men, women, and children into extreme situations of indentured servitude and bondage. During that period of enormous industrial expansion, children provided very cheap and obedient labor while incurring almost no expenses to factory owners. Today, the same high demand for child labor exists in the manufacturing industries of India and other South Asian countries.

Outside the U.S., selling or loaning children was acceptable for poor families less than one hundred years ago. In China, for example, boys and girls known as *mui tsai* were purchased by rich families as domestic servants, often working for the same family until death. And in Haiti, where child servants to this day are referred to as *restaveks,* poor rural families routinely send their children to the city to work as unpaid domestics in households only slightly better off than themselves.

While the practice has gone on for years, many people believe the transportation and exploitation of children to be a new issue simply because the phrase "child trafficking" has only recently entered the vernacular. In the earlier years of the 20th century, *trafficking,* to the general public, usually referred to the smuggling of guns or later to "rum-running" during Prohibition. More recently *trafficking* referred mostly to the smuggling of illegal drugs. References to "human trafficking," "trafficking in women and children," and "child trafficking" entered the public awareness in the late 1980s.

While the phrase "child trafficking" itself emphasizes the illicit transportation of children, it also carries the inextricable link to their inevitable exploitation. After 1900, European governments grew concerned about the recruitment of young women and girls into prostitution in foreign countries. They began to develop several international treaties which sought to end what they referred to as the "White Slave Trade" and later "White Slave Traffic."

By the 1930s, the English version of these treaties used the word "traffic" in reference to the exploitation, while French, Spanish and other languages referred to it with the word "trade." This caused confusion over terminology which continues today. However, after the Second World War until the 1980s, the term "trafficking" generally referred to exploitation of young women and girls into prostitution. Since prostitution was a crime in most places where the trafficking took place, the girls recruited into the trade were considered to be trafficking victims whether or not they entered consensually or against their will.

During the 1990s government and human rights organizations around the world began to realize that girls and boys were being moved in large numbers in order to be exploited in various ways, all for profit. This gave new meaning to child trafficking; the meaning we have today. In 2002 The United Nations' report, *Abolishing Slavery and its Contemporary Forms,* states that "The trafficking of persons today can be viewed as the modern equivalent of the slave trade of the nineteenth century."

* * *

The slavery of children today takes on many terrible forms. Former Secretary of State Colin Powell declared, "The more you learn about how the most innocent and vulnerable among us are savaged by these crimes, the more impossible it becomes to look the other way. Women and girls as young as six years old are being trafficked into commercial sexual exploitation; men are being trafficked into forced labor; children are being trafficked into war as child soldiers."

In general, child trafficking takes place in order to sell young people into:

- **Exploitation through sex**. The most predominant manifestation of child trafficking. This includes forced prostitution and pornography in dangerous and filthy conditions.
- **Exploitation through work**. This includes slave labor or bonded labor on plantations, households, mines, construction, sweat shops or in some cases life-threatening sporting activities.
- **Exploitation through illegal activity**. This includes begging, drug trafficking, theft, and often violence against others.
- **Child Soldering**. Very young people, mostly boys, are forced to perform the worst and most dangerous activities in armed conflicts around the world.
- **The Adoption Trade**. There is a worldwide market illegally providing children to families desperate enough to purchase a stolen or abandoned child.
- **Supplying body parts**. This is not science fiction or an urban legend. It is a living nightmare and a growing problem that will only increase as medical science advances its ability to save and extend life.
- **Bride Selling and Forced Marriage**. In many cultures, female life holds little value. Families will rid themselves of a young daughter by selling her into a marriage of abuse and servitude.

* * *

Svetlana was a young girl from Belarus who was living in Minsk and looking for a job in order to send money back home. During her search, she came upon some Turkish men who promised her a well-paying job in Istanbul. The money and work sounded very good. Svetlana agreed. The moment she crossed the border, her passport and money were taken and she was locked in an old apartment building high above the city streets. There Svetlana and another girl were forced into prostitution. After several weeks, Svetlana tried to escape. She jumped out of a window and fell six stories to the street below.

According to Turkish court documents, customers did not take Svetlana to the hospital, they called the traffickers instead, who took what was left of her life. Svetlana's body lay unclaimed in the morgue for two weeks until Turkish authorities learned her identity and sent her body to Belarus.

Source: U.S. State Department

The most prevalent use of trafficked children is sexual exploitation. Child traffickers typically target young girls and boys who live in poverty or have difficult family relationships. Defenseless and intimidated by the unfamiliar surroundings, they cannot fight against the persons exploiting them. Should they attempt to do so, they are forced into submission.

Traffickers are known to recruit their victims using a variety of methods. While abduction and kidnapping is often their tool, trafficking victims are very often trapped in more subversive ways. Typically, the traffickers promise their victims, usually girls and young women, that they will have respectable work as waitresses or domestic servants in another country.

Traffickers may also persuade parents that their children will have a better life elsewhere: a secure job and the chance of a better education and future. In fact, they are literally selling them to hidden and dirty brothels. Some of these parents or girls may even know, or suspect, that they will be sex workers, but desperate poverty and lack of both education and awareness lead them to accept any offer, no matter what the risk may be.

What they do not know is the extent of the abuse and degradation they will suffer, and the likelihood that they will be held captive for the remainder of their lives. In any case, they go with these strangers only to discover upon their arrival in some strange land that they are victims of an evil deception. Like millions of others, they become slaves.

Further, children forced to work in the sex industry are at considerable risk of contracting sexually transmitted diseases, including HIV/AIDS. For girls, there is the added risk of very early pregnancy and permanent damage to their reproductive health.

Some trafficked children are also subdued and controlled with drugs to which they become easily addicted. They are then completely trapped within the cycle of exploitation because continuing with the work is believed to be the only way to satisfy their drug addictions.

* * *

The various manifestations of child trafficking and the exploitations children face today are significantly different from the past. These differences have led to an explosion in children being exploited worldwide for a number of reasons:

Children can be transported easily. Adults can move children quickly and inexpensively by air to countries where they are in demand. For example, very young boys are often flown from Bangladesh, India, Pakistan and Sudan to airports in Persian Gulf countries. Carrying false documents identifying them as other people's children, they are sold to be jockeys for camel races

There is an increased demand for children for sexual exploitation. People with enough financial resources can easily travel to far off countries only to buy sex with young people. These are not just pedophiles. The fear of HIV/AIDS motivates men to pay for sex with very young girls assuming they are less likely to have the disease than adults.

The internet allows anonymous communication among those offering and seeking sex with children. Along with making it easier for sex tourists to operate, the internet has also fueled shocking increases in child pornography and "mail order brides."

There is an increasing demand for very low-wage labor. As the world becomes one global consumer market place, inexpensive labor is needed to supply the demand for cheaper products. As wages decrease, child workers are needed by the millions because they are the cheapest and most malleable work force available.

* * *

This problem is not small or simple. It is a looming threat to children in poverty everywhere. Actress Julia Ormond is the UN Goodwill Ambassador to combat human trafficking and slavery. During testimony before the Global Human Rights and International Operations Subcommittee of the U.S. Congress, she stated, "I have been horrified by the extent of the problem, the searing depth of the experience of the victims, and the extraordinary level of profit to the traffickers."

Clearly, the situation for children victimized by trafficking is extremely serious. This is aggravated by a completely inadequate level of response by law enforcement agencies in many key countries and the absence of any coordinated policing at the international level. Ms. Ormond, who has traveled to several countries meeting with trafficking victims, continued her testimony by saying, "Governments and member states need to rise to the challenge of making this issue a priority and work together, without shaming and blaming, to create the structure that recognizes the extremity of this issue."

Child trafficking, while hiding in the shadows, is not discreet. It involves many people coordinating a complex series of connected events that take place in the home of the child, along transit routes and at final destinations. Exploitation begins as soon as the child is taken by the trafficker, occurring at the beginning, middle and end of the trafficking process. At its core, *Child trafficking occurs whenever a child is relocated and exploited.* That means anyone who contributes to the process: recruiters, middlemen, document providers, drivers, corrupt officials, employers and service providers, are *traffickers.*

Financial profit is always the motive of traffickers. Children simply become another product to be supplied to waiting customers. This abomination is a multi-billion dollar international trade in which millions of people make money from the flesh of children who are sold to the highest bidder. In their greed these criminals reduce all of humanity by weaving the enslavement of innocents into the fabric of society.

In the end, no matter what amount of money is trading hands, the children are paying the highest price.

* * *

Five

I am Hanna

A Glut of Slaves

* * *

"I was moved around by these people, to different places. In Romania, I had eight clients a day; in Turkey, four or five a day; and in Spain, ten. In the United Kingdom, probably twelve. Of course some of the clients beat you. This is how they treat you. They don't care if you live or die. They just do not want to get caught. So, I took an overdose, I tried to hang myself, I tried to jump off a balcony. If I died they get another girl to replace what I am doing. It is easy for them. There are so many girls. So many."

Hanna, 13
Source: UNICEF

* * *

Between 1918 and 1959, 66 million men, women, and children were trafficked to slave labor concentration camps within Russia. "Slave labor made no demands, could be transferred anywhere at any moment, was free of family ties, had no need for housing, schools or hospitals, and sometimes not even for kitchens or lavatories. The state could obtain such manpower only by swallowing up its sons," wrote Nobel Prize winner Alexander Solzhenitsyn in his landmark 1974 book, *The Gulag Archipelago.* Often referred to as a "nation of camps," the slave-labor system was located over vast stretches of land across Siberia and was a major factor in the development of the Soviet Union as a super power.

Today, the Gulags are empty. Most of the millions who suffered and froze through decades of forced labor within them are gone. With their passing ended the last massive, state-sponsored system of enslavement and forced labor on earth. Even their legacy has vanished; for the nightmare of so many did not rid the world of slavery.

Human bondage has changed since Solzhenitsyn, a victim of the Gulag himself, revealed to the world what the Soviet Union had done. It has changed, but it has not improved. The victims involved have multiplied and the profits have increased. The methods of moving people have become more sophisticated. The products they are forced to produce are of higher quality and meant for the international market. The wars they are forced to fight are more brutal and deadly. The children are much younger.

According to the FBI, human trafficking generates $12 billion internationally each year. The International Labor Organization (ILO) has conducted far more detailed studies and estimates the number is $32 billion. They also estimate, along with the United Nations, that there are more slaves today than any other time in history. Together, they calculate 27 million men, women, children, *and* babies, are enslaved today. And the number is growing.

* * *

"Several crucial differences in the slaves of the old days were that they were expensive, you kept them for their whole lives, and you took excellent care of them. Today, they are cheap. In fact, there is a glut of slaves and when you've used them, you throw them away if you don't want them anymore. They're disposable."

Dr. Kevin Bales
Director, Free The Slaves

* * *

Because the global exploitation of children is well hidden in the shadows of every society, there is no way to determine exactly how many children are victimized each year. The most respected calculations are determined by the ILO and are the most often cited by governments and human rights organizations. In 2002, the ILO's Program for the Elimination of Child Labor estimated that out of a total of 8.4 million boys and girls engaged in what they refer to as the "unconditional worst forms of child labor," 1.2 million had been trafficked. Today, the ILO calculates that up to two million children each year are victims of child trafficking. Yet, even the ILO says this number is probably very low.

Dr. Kevin Bales, Director of the international organization *Free The Slaves*, is considered one of the world's leading experts on contemporary slavery. During their research, his dedicated staff "discovered a shocking world that harbors brothels filled with kidnapped women and girls enslaved in prostitution, of wealthy households that victimize women and girls in forced domestic servitude and sex, of young children living in cages beside their workplace."

The extent to which the slavery of children covers the map is astounding. It is "found on every continent except Antarctica. Migrant agriculture slavery flourishes in every nation alongside greed, debt bondage, servile marriage contracts, and garment sweatshop factories," Bales says. It is always difficult to build hard statistical information pertaining to any a clandestine activity. Most countries have no specific legislation against trafficking, and victims are reluctant to report their experiences for fear of being prosecuted and deported as illegal immigrants.

The U.S. Department of State provides another commonly cited statistic, conservatively estimating that 800,000 to 900,000 people worldwide, mainly women and children, are trafficked each year. However, this is universally seen as an underestimate. The UN now believes that the number of children trafficked annually, within nations and across borders is around 1.2 million. Further data from both sources reveal that eighty percent of the victims trafficked across international borders are female and seventy percent end up as slaves in brutal sexual exploitation of various types.

When these and other statistics are calculated, they usually refer only to children who have been trafficked across international borders, and not children trafficked within their own countries. Some estimates that include global intra-country human trafficking range from two to four million. Fortunately, thanks to very detailed data painstakingly obtained by ILO's Program for the Elimination of Child Labor and UNICEF, there is a clearer picture of what child trafficking leads to in specific areas of the world.

In *Sri Lanka*, children often become the prey of sexual exploiters through friends and relatives. The prevalence of boys in prostitution there is fueled by foreign tourism.

An estimated 12,000 *Nepalese* children, mainly girls, are trafficked for sexual commercial exploitation each year within Nepal or to brothels in India and other countries.

Some eighty-four percent of girls in prostitution interviewed in *Tanzania* reported having been battered, raped or tortured by police officers and local community guards, who are really nothing more than thugs. Some of these girls started out as child domestic workers and at least sixty percent of them had no permanent place to live.

In *El Salvador*, one-third of the sexually exploited children between fourteen and seventeen years of age are boys. Among all children interviewed, the median age for entering into prostitution was thirteen years. Most worked five days per week, although nearly ten percent reported that they worked seven days a week.

In *Vietnam*, family poverty, low family education and family dysfunction cause widespread commercial sexual exploitation of children. Sixty-six percent of the children involved in prostitution reported that tuition and school fees were beyond the means of their families' income.

While a complete picture is not possible, these examples partially illustrate what is happening *within nations* throughout the world.

* * *

"What a lot of people don't realize is that in some countries it's not just that the police and government don't have child prostitution on the top of their list, it also happens that if kids who are forced into it run away from the pimps, a lot of times the police actually track them down and take them back (to the brothels), because it's such a good business, and they themselves get discounts for 'helping out.'"

Rita, 15
Source: International Labor Organization

* * *

While the exact number of trafficking victims found throughout the world is inherently difficult to produce, human trafficking, like drug trafficking and arms smuggling, is even harder to quantify because of the many forms it takes. Child slavery is common on the farms of India, the debt-bondage brick-making kilns of Pakistan, the cocoa plantations of Cote d'Ivoire, and the rug loom sheds of Nepal. It is increasing exponentially in the sex-slavery brothels of Manila, Thailand, Ecuador, Japan and the U.S.; the water-carrier chattel in Mauritania; and the charcoal-making camps of Brazil. It is cheered at camel races where young boys ride for the pleasure of wealthy Sheikhs in United Arab Emirates, Saudi Arabia, Kuwait and Qatar. Closer to the west, slavery exists in the garment sweatshops of Los Angeles and New York, in the sex clubs of Cleveland and Detroit, and in the secret world of domestic servitude in the wealthiest homes in Zurich, London, Dallas and Washington, D.C.

The problem of calculating its extent is made even more complex because available data on trafficking varies considerably from region to region. For example, there is "a noted paucity of data, for example, of persons trafficked to, from, or through the Middle East," states a report by the U.S. State Department.

Fortunately, the UN and the ILO have formed a partnership in order to study the exploitation of children wherever it exists. Their data as it pertains to sexual exploitation has concluded that it "happens all over the world: in rich countries and in poor; in many different locations, including on the street, in brothels, in private homes, and in tourist facilities, such as hotels." Among their findings the report found that:

- There are between 40,000 and 60,000 children in prostitution in the Taiwan Province of China;
- Twenty-five percent of all people in prostitution in Tulear, Madagascar, are children;
- In the United States, one in five children who use the internet regularly are approached by strangers for sex;
- In Mexico, more than 16,000 children are involved in prostitution. Mexico is the number one center for the supply of young children to North America. The majority of these children over the age of twelve end up becoming prostitutes;
- In Lithuania, twenty to fifty percent of people in prostitution are children. Children as young as eleven are known to work in brothels and some children between ten and twelve years old have been used to make pornographic films;
- Although the majority of victims of child sexual exploitation are female, the percentage of boys who are suffering is increasing dramatically. Traditionally, abuse and exploitation of boys has been less reported than that of girls. In Sri Lanka alone, there are between 5,000 and 30,000 Sri Lankan boys in prostitution who are used by Western sex tourists;
- In the Dominican Republic and Haiti, boys reportedly stay with adult male tourists on the beaches.

A few other organizations, studying the issue of child trafficking closely since the late 1990s, strive to shed what light they can on the topic. Thomas Miller, Executive Director of Plan, an international organization working to improve the lives of deprived children, found that the internet makes it possible for "girls as young as thirteen to be trafficked from Asia and Eastern Europe as 'mail-order brides' for customers in the West."

Perhaps, with the irresistible globalization of the late 20th century, the international scope of child trafficking was inevitable. Since 1990, porous borders and improved communications have made the business far more successful for traffickers, bringing the trade to unprecedented levels. For example:

- Immigration controls at the border between Paraguay and Brazil are very difficult to patrol because of the terrain, allowing children to be easily trafficked in both directions;
- Since border officials usually do not require identification papers from unaccompanied children or from children traveling with adults, girls are trafficked from Thailand to South Africa via Singapore, while children from several African nations are trafficked to South East Asia via South Africa;
- In Greece, more than forty percent of the children working as prostitutes are from countries which can be reached by car, such as Uzbekistan, Kazakhstan, Armenia, Albania and Iraq.

* * *

"I maintain that one of the worst new evils of the last two decades, truly satanic, is the attack on children. Those of Beslan, of Iraq, of Egypt; Palestinian and Israeli children. Or the innocent child soldiers in Africa. There is no longer hope or trust in the future of children, and in these events you see this as in a mirror."

Rowan Williams
The Archbishop of Canterbury

* * *

Looking beyond the data, it is easy to discover the wide scope of exploitation throughout the world. Child trafficking in all its forms is exploding. The slavery of children on a large scale is no longer confined to Asia or Africa. It is thriving everywhere. In fact, a United Kingdom vice squad detective stated that child trafficking is like "a slow tidal wave moving westward."

While statistics certainly provide a better understanding of the concept of child trafficking as it exists today, the issue is not numerically based. It is based on the lives of children and the reality "that trafficking and slavery most often involves violence, beatings, and murder committed by world-organized crime lords, pimps, and traffickers," says Kevin Bales.

From all corners of the globe children are swept up in the slave trade. Millions of them are used as fuel for the fires of every human evil. This glut of slaves comes from every race and culture; they do not look alike or speak the same languages. They are moved from country to country and town to town for a multitude of perversions. Yet, they all have one thing in common: *they are worthless to the world.* For if the world did not find them worthless, then every decent citizen of every nation on earth would rise up and demand that each child be saved.

So far, there is only silence.

In that silence, imagine for a moment you are that child. You have known fear, hatred, violence and abandonment. Alone, you wait, not knowing what abuse you will face next. The only thing you know for sure is that no one is coming to help you. Your hope is gone. You expect the misery to continue. Pain is normal. The dread you experience is in knowing that the world has other priorities, and that you have been forgotten.

* * *

Six

I am Diane

A Cancer Spreading Across the World

* * *

"Diane Piiliv, aged 29, was last seen entering a car, possibly a taxi, outside Club Alcatraz in downtown Helsinki early on the morning of June 9, 2006. Male voices were heard from inside the car. Piiliv had been spending the night in the club with her lady friends. The missing female is a witness who was to have an important role in an upcoming trial involving trafficking in humans. The woman is one of the plaintiffs, or victims, in the case. It is possible that there is a link between her disappearance and the upcoming trial as her testimony would be important to the trial's successful prosecution."

Sorce: Helsinki, Finland Police Report

* * *

Diane completely disappeared.

According to Helsinki Detective Chief Inspector Seppo Sillanpää, "It is hard evidence against certain human trafficking suspects because it is unusual that a witness goes missing just before a major trial."

It was obvious to everyone that she did not vanish on her own. Diane Piiliv called her family every day without fail. She also didn't have much money with her. Nor did the border police report anyone using her passport trying to leave the country. Finally, the police tried to trace her mobile phone usage. There hasn't been any.

She's just gone.

The trial in which Piiliv was to testify charges eight people with aggravated human trafficking. The suspects were all in custody and separated from each other when she went missing.

* * *

While not a child, Diane Piiliv remains a victim of organized crime's global human trafficking underworld. No longer even referred to as organized crime by most law enforcement agencies, having gone international in their activities and ultra-sophisticated in their operations, these syndicates now comprise what is now called *transnational crime.*

They come from every nation and speak every language. They will gladly work with their sworn national or ideological enemies to make the kind of money available in the trading of human flesh and other crimes. They have no loyalty to anyone. They use death and torture regularly. And they are making child trafficking the fastest growing crime in the world.

What makes children such an attractive business? Consider that a drug can only be sold once. Likewise, a gun can only be sold once. But, you can sell the living body of a child over and over and over again, making a profit every time.

Without regard to the pain and suffering they bring to innocent children, the profits are too high for international criminals to resist. Pedophiliac customers all over the world are willing to pay any cost to satisfy their fantasies and desires. So crime syndicates from Africa, Asia, Europe, and the Americas do whatever it takes to meet the demand.

Anyone who gets in their way, like Diane Piiliv, just disappears.

This author firmly believes that no one has yet written a book focusing exclusively on child trafficking because of the inherent dangers in exposing the dark criminal enterprise which propagates it worldwide. These operations have much to lose if the people of the world become aware of what they are doing. They are making enormous amounts of money operating in the shadows of our society. Anyone who shines light into the places they hide is doing so at tremendous risk.

No matter. It's time we turn on the lights.

* * *

"A trafficker recruited Nina, a nineteen-year-old from southeastern Europe, to work as a waitress, but then raped, beat, and drugged her, forcing her into prostitution. After a daring escape, her trafficker hunted her down and kidnapped her. Taken into custody during a police raid, Nina agreed to be a witness against her trafficker. The police officer assigned to protect her gave away her location and her trafficker threatened her life. At the trial, she was forced to sit next to her traffickers and was insulted and humiliated by the judge and defense counsel. Her pimps were found guilty but released on appeal. For her own survival, Nina has fled to another country and assumed a new identity."

Former Secretary of State Colin Powell

* * *

Transnational crime syndicates are vast and vicious. They are not the criminals of *The Godfather* or *The Sopranos*. In fact, these modern-day slave traders make the crimes of Don Vito Corleone seem quaint. Dr. Louise I. Shelley, founder and Director of the Terrorism, Transnational Crime and Corruption Center at American University, sees that "transnational crime will be a defining issue of the 21st century for policymakers, as defining as the Cold War was for the 20th century and colonialism was for the 19th. Terrorists and transnational crime groups will proliferate because these crime groups are major beneficiaries of globalization. They take advantage of increased travel, trade, rapid money movements, telecommunications and computer links, and are well positioned for growth."

Dr. Shelley, in an opinion shared by many in the international community, points to the global and diverse influence of organized crime on terrorism which allows them operate effectively across and above national borders. "No one country defending (itself) alone against them can be assured international and homeland security or safety from terrorist organizations with criminal links. Organized crime groups are involved in an eclectic array of activities ranging from trafficking in human beings, to the illegal sales of weapons, narcotics, nuclear material, and money laundering to hide the proceeds from these illicit industries."

In the past, crime syndicates directed illegal activities such as drug trafficking, prostitution, illegal gambling, loan-sharking and extortion. They typically controlled specific geographic territories, did not usually attempt to operate outside their spheres of influence and only rarely cooperated with other syndicates. Until the 1970s, a traditional Sicilian-based crime family would require permission to conduct business in another family's zone even if it were only a block away.

Today, organized crime is no longer limited to street-level activity. Transnational crime has entered the global market and they model their practices on multi-national corporations. They have become contemporary organizations that "are adaptable, sophisticated, extremely opportunistic and immersed in a full range of illegal and legal activities. While still involved at the lower level . . . they have expanded their activities to a quasi-corporate level where they are active in large-scale insurance fraud, the depletion of natural resources, environmental crime, migrant smuggling, bank fraud, gasoline tax fraud and corruption," states Jim Judd, Director of The Canadian Security Intelligence Service.

Transnational organized crime groups may have profited the most from globalization in all its forms. After all, legitimate businesses are constrained by domestic and home country laws and regulations. Through corruption, blackmail, and intimidation, international criminal networks use open markets and open societies to their full advantage.

Of course, they never hesitate to use violence or murder to obtain greater market share and financial objectives. They are also very willing to work within any country where legal or bureaucratic loopholes provide the best advantage. And similar to legitimate international corporations, modern criminal organizations are very willing to work together, often bartering for the use of each other's resources to accomplish specific tasks, or to enter long term agreement when it suits their needs.

* * *

"Transnational organized crime has been likened to a cancer, spreading across the world. It can undermine democracy, disrupt free markets, drain national assets, and inhibit the development of stable societies. In doing so, national and international criminal groups threaten the security of all nations."

Paula Dobriansky
U.S. Under Secretary of State for Global Affairs

* * *

Despite all this new activity, the traditional markets of drug and weapon trafficking remain the two largest activities for all international crime syndicates. The fact that child trafficking is a gaining momentum at number three cannot be overstated. By far the most profitable for international criminals, trafficking of children has three distinct advantages over their dealings in drugs and weapons.

One, it requires *less investment* than either illegal drugs or weapons. Young people can be obtained anywhere in the world with little or no money. Early coercion of victims often leads to a situation where the trafficker is being paid to take possession of them.

Two, children are much *easier to move.* Drugs and weapons must be hidden, often requiring sophisticated, complex and expensive methods of invisible transportation. Children can be successfully and quickly moved in plain sight. A sleeping child or two in the backseat of a car is a common sight at border crossings.

Three, children can be sold *multiple times.* Children forced into prostitution can be made to service several clients every day.

Increasing the scope of business even further, several new trends in transnational crime have made their foray into child trafficking even more successful.

Cyber-crime is a powerful weapon in the modern criminals' arsenal and is expected to bring them increasing power and profit in the years to come. Along with their extensive use of the internet to locate available children and promote child pornography, the growth of global, computerized financial networks has allowed underworld organizations to launder illegal profits quickly and easily via global transactions that are instantaneous and virtually untraceable. The United Nations estimates that at least $200 billion in drug money is hidden or moved every year largely through the use of international electronic bank transfers.

Further, they are able to access almost any information in the world using computer hackers and other computer savvy experts to steal cyber-information. Criminals at this level do not need to develop technical expertise about the internet. They simply hire the best hackers who have the specific expertise or security knowledge they need, or they make contact with employees of whatever organization they are attempting to raid and bribe them to become inside hackers. Using rewards and threats, the hackers are properly motivated to carry out their assigned tasks effectively and efficiently.

Legitimization allows transnational criminals to distance themselves from the illegal aspects of their operations by investing in legitimate business ventures. Legitimate businesses can be used to hide or launder cash or to simply give the criminal a positive image. These upfront businesses do not have to be successful or even try to be since they are funded by the enormous profits acquired through underground criminal activities. Legitimacy can also be had through donations to charities, hospitals, universities and political causes. Instead of lurking in the shadows away from the spotlight, some prefer to hide in plain sight, even hiring international public relations firms in order to boost their status in the world's view. "The detection and neutralization of transnational organized crime groups become even more difficult because these groups tend to use legitimate import-export firms, service industries, or even multinational financial institutions as cover for their activities," states Pino Arlacchi, Executive Director, United Nations Office for Drug Control and Crime Prevention. "Sometimes the criminal organization only nests itself inside a larger business; at other times it actually controls it. The border line between the activities of white collar or corporate crime on the one hand and transnational organized crime on the other is often fuzzy," Arlacchi points out.

Cooperation among diverse transnational crime organizations, already a major factor in the new *under*world order, continues to expand, making them more effective and difficult to fight. If it were not for their illegal activities, the extensive cooperation among them would be enviable examples of cross-cultural, international, and multi-discipline partnerships among common business interests. Detailed financial agreements, bartering arrangements and strong resource alliances allow syndicates to evade law enforcement, share existing infrastructure, exchange intelligence and information, and improve risk management. For instance, "Albanian organized crime groups have formed partnerships with the Gambino, Genovese, and Luchese La Cosa Nostra families to facilitate specific crimes," stated Grant D. Ashley, Assistant Director, Criminal Investigative Division of the FBI.

Sophistication, already a superior quality of transnational crime, is increasing to unprecedented levels. Some professionals working within the organizations have major university degrees in business, accounting and law. With talented human resources they are extremely well equipped to operate and take advantage of the complex world of transnational crime. "For organized crime, this influx of professional intelligence, police, and military know-how has meant a quantum jump in sophistication. Crime groups can in certain cases outsmart the police because they have better technique, better equipment, and more resources," says Pino Arlacchi.

* * *

"The powerful Russian Solntsevskaya and Ismailovskaya criminal enterprises are involved in all types of criminal activity in the United States, from drug trafficking and human trafficking to burglary and home invasion robbery rings, from money laundering and securities fraud to traditional organized crime gambling and extortion rackets.

The Sicilian mafia is not alone in Italian organized crime groups which also include the Neapolitan Camorra, and the Calabrian-Ndrangheta among others. Collectively they have evolved from kidnappings for ransom to drug trafficking and the systemic corruption of public officials to gain lucrative municipal contracts. The Puglian Sacra Corona Unita is taking advantage of its geographic proximity to the Balkans to align itself with Balkan organized criminal groups engaged in arms and cigarette smuggling, trafficking in humans, and alien smuggling.

European nations have recognized that Balkan organized crime is one of the greatest criminal threats that they face. European police organizations now estimate that Balkan organized crime groups control upwards of seventy percent of the heroin market in some of the larger European nations, and are rapidly taking over human smuggling, prostitution and car theft rings across Europe."

From the Testimony of Grant D. Ashley,
Assistant Director, Criminal Investigative Division, FBI
Before the Subcommittee on European Affairs,
Committee on Foreign Relations, United States Senate

* * *

The methods used by organized crime to exploit children are effective, creative and ruthless. Everything they do is designed to deceive and coerce their victims into giving their full confidence to the trafficker. Once they have gained control of the child's life there is virtually no escape. The criminals' motive is profit and absolutely no tolerance is given to obstacles.

Their efficiency is startling. Jamtala Daspara, a village in the West Bengal region of India, is an excellent example of their operational efficiency. The village does not have any teenage girls.

The complete absence of girls in this small village is an extreme but telling case of a trend that is occurring across the world: young girls in poor villages are being tricked or sold into the sex trade through false promises of marriage, education, and offers of money to help their families.

Of course, the problem is not isolated to rural areas or tiny villages. Look closely enough at any poverty-stricken region of the word, rural or urban, and you will find child traffickers seeking product for their trade.

It takes the professional administration of money, people and communications, to organize a crime perpetrated across national borders in a post-9/11 world. Large organized crime groups control growing sectors of child trafficking in China, Colombia, Japan, and Vietnam. Along with the crime groups listed previously in the quote by FBI Assistant Director Grant D. Ashley, these crime groups often wield significant political power through corruption and extortion, and are known for their use of extreme violence.

Chinese - The Tongs and Triad have been involved in human trafficking as well as the more traditional crimes of drug smuggling, gambling, and prostitution in cities across the world. The Tongs are an older and very secretive society, dating back to the 1800s. The Triads acquired their name from the British due to their fascination with numerology, the importance of the number three, and their mystical initiation ceremonies. They believe it is their destiny to control all vice activity. The Wah Ching is a Chinese criminal organization involved in trafficking, murder, extortion, prostitution, robbery, gambling, and loan sharking. The Wo Hop To Triad is a well established criminal organization originating in Hong Kong. These groups began immigrating to the United States, mostly California, during the mid-1980s. They have a long history of involvement in trafficking, prostitution, narcotics, illegal gambling and extortion.

Colombian - Drugs are not the only illegal product of the Cartels. The Colombian crime syndicates tend to have many sympathizers and work within a very complex infrastructure with up to 24,000 people in one organization. The organized crime networks, some related to terrorist organizations, promote child sex tourism, especially in Cartagena and resort areas on the Caribbean coast. Colombian children are also trafficked to South, Central, and North America, the Caribbean, Western Europe, Japan, Hong Kong, and the Middle East.

Japanese - The Yakuza, with origins dating back to the seventh century, are at the very core of Asian organized crime. They are responsible for "women and children primarily trafficked to Japan from Thailand, the Philippines, Russia, and Eastern Europe for commercial sexual exploitation," according to the U.S. State Department, which goes on to say that, on a smaller scale, "women and children are trafficked from Colombia, Brazil, Mexico, South Korea, Malaysia, Burma, and Indonesia for sexual servitude."

Vietnamese - The operations and influence of Vietnamese origin is growing since some of the Vietnamese gang members are being recruited by Asian organized crime groups such as the Wah Ching and the Wo Hop To Triad in the San Francisco and Los Angeles areas. They are considered by many to be the most ruthless of the Asian gangs involved in all aspects of child trafficking.

* * *

Without organized transnational crime, the world would not have experienced the horrible growth of child trafficking. These organizations are fundamental to the increasing problem of children being abused, tortured and killed for profit. They have assembled intricate systems of operation to build the criminal networks capable of sustaining this business. It will take an even greater assembly of organization, dedication, intelligence and passion to fight them.

The international syndicates responsible for these atrocities against children cannot be stopped by any one individual or group or nation. It will require millions of people from every country working together with utter devotion to the one goal of keeping every child safe from the hands of traffickers and customers.

The underworld has started a war against children and, for the most part, we have not been fighting back. Until now it has been a secret war that was easy to ignore, but no longer.

The secret is out. The war is on.

* * *

As of this writing, Diane Piiliv has not been located.

Diane Piiliv is about 160 cm tall and has long black hair, and she is of average build. One of her front teeth is broken. She was last seen wearing black jeans, a blue top, a dark blouse, and a pair of canvas boots with high heels. The Helsinki Criminal Police requests any information concerning Diane Piiliv be directed to their offices by calling (09) 189 5464 or (09) 189 4002.

* * *

Seven

I am Masha

My Secret

* * *

Masha was born in southern Russia. When she was four years old, her mother took a knife and stabbed her in the back of her neck during a drinking binge. With no father, Masha was sent to live in an orphanage. It was a sad and desperate existence, but one day, a divorced 41-year-old American came to the orphanage and wanted to adopt her.
Matthew Mancuso found Masha through an adoption agency in Cherry Hill, N.J. He said he wanted to adopt a young Caucasian girl. He picked Masha from a videotape sent to him by the adoption agency. At first, Mancuso was kind and bought Masha gifts. The nightmare began when Masha flew home with Mancuso to his modest, middle-class house near Pittsburgh. When it was time for bed on her first night in America, he didn't send her to her room. He told her to get in bed with him. "He wasn't wearing any clothes. The first couple of nights, he touched my legs and chest. Then he started touching my private parts," Masha recalls. A few days later, he started raping her repeatedly. Then he started taking sexually explicit photographs of her. "I'd make myself think of other things when it was happening," she said. "He'd tell me not to tell anyone, or else something bad would happen," Masha says. "He wouldn't tell me what it would be, but he'd just say something bad would happen. So I just didn't tell anybody, 'cause I was afraid."

Source: ABC News

* * *

The very thought of children being abused in such a way, only to create images for the sexual fantasies of others, is so completely abhorrent that most of us dismiss the issue entirely. Certainly, the words "child" and "pornography" should never be placed anywhere near each other. Yet, the very phrase, *child pornography*, calls to mind scenes which a healthy, functioning adult can not imagine. In fact, the criminals who are using children for sexual images and the predators paying to view them are all hoping the public continues to turn away from child pornography. They are depending on us to ignore it so that they never have to stop.

While it is extremely difficult to examine the issue of child pornography, it is not necessary to see the images or even imagine them. It only takes courage to look at this growing, worldwide phenomenon for what it is: a criminal act which exploits enslaved children.

It may be easy to keep some aspects of child trafficking at a distance. It can be dismissed as something that occurs to other people from other cultures in other countries. Contrary to what most would like to believe, all forms of child sexual exploitation do not exist exclusively at a convenient distance.

Child pornography is fast, cheap, easy and as close as the nearest computer. Usually defined as an illegal form of pornography, involving minors in video or still images, child pornography is a multi-billion dollar industry.* Even with legislation enacted during the last few years, making it a serious crime to possess sexual images of children, the proliferation of child pornography has not slowed. In fact, it is exploding everywhere on the web. While the internet "is one of the greatest inventions of the last century," said Alice Fisher, Assistant Attorney General in testimony before the U.S. Senate, "unfortunately, it has also largely contributed to the exacerbation of the child pornography epidemic."

A U.S. Justice Department report, *Project Safe Childhood*, carefully studied sexual offenses committed against children. It determined that, "judging simply by crime statistics, it is clear that the internet is helping to fuel an epidemic of child pornography."

* There are almost no reliable statistics or numbers pertaining to the actual dollar amount spent on child pornography. Because of the illegal nature of this industry, any reported numbers would be vague estimates at best. However, sources from the FBI to the *New York Times* have placed the figure anywhere from $3 to $20 billion annually.

The report explains that by providing greater technical ease and increased anonymity in trading images, the internet has "taken down barriers that at one time served as a deterrent to child pornographers."

In 2003, an estimated 20,000 images of child pornography were posted on the internet each week. Between 1998 and 2004, child-pornography reports made to the National Center for Missing and Exploited Children increased from 3,267 to 106,119; a 30-fold increase over a six-year period. The Justice Department also noted that there has been an escalation in the severity of abuse depicted in child pornography in recent years, "with the images found today more frequently involving younger children, including toddlers and even infants."

"I think it is fair to say children are in more danger than ever before from child exploitation," states Drew Oosterbaan, chief of the Justice Department's Child Exploitation and Obscenity Section. "We see child pornography escalating, not just in terms of numbers, not just in the amount or frequency of distribution of child pornography we see, but most especially in the nature of the child pornography we see," he explains, noting that there are more images of children being violently raped and abused. In her testimony before the U.S. Senate, Alice Fisher explained that "these offenders often compete to see who can produce the most unthinkable photos or videos of raping and molesting children, the internet has led to the victimization of younger and younger children. These images make your stomach turn. Images have been produced, for example, of young toddlers, including one in which a baby is tied up with towels, desperately crying in pain, while she is being brutally raped and sodomized by an adult man. Likewise, videos are being circulated of very young daughters forced to have intercourse and oral sex with their fathers."

Everything surrounding this material is illegal from the act of creating them to the images themselves. "Most images today of child pornography depict actual sexual abuse of real children. Each image literally documents a crime scene," explained U.S. Attorney General Alberto Gonzales in a recent speech.

In a study conducted by *The New York Times*, more than 200 sites, aimed at pedophiles, focus mostly on one specific child on each. Almost all the children appear to be between the ages of 2 and 12 and are photographed by people who have frequent access to them. The sites often include images of "guests," children who are described as a friend of the featured child, but who appear for only a day. The sites claim the children are from different parts of the world, including the United States.

The purveyors of these images are extremely sophisticated in the use of computers and talented in their manipulation of children. What they produce is in growing demand by online predators who seek to purchase child pornography. It is an amicable and efficient partnership of abuser and predator, seller and buyer, with children caught in the middle.

* * *

"Feel her breathe on your face, take a gentle touch from your screen, open your mind and push the limits. Only 9 years old! Hot!"

Source: PlayToy.com

* * *

Those who supply child pornography on the web and those who purchase it there, are not alone in this conspiracy against children. Many others are complicit and many of us know and interact with them every day.

It takes an enormous digital and corporate infrastructure to make the internet function as it does, especially when commerce is conducted online. Reputable companies like Dell, Hewlett Packard, Microsoft, AOL, MasterCard, Visa, Paypal, Amazon, Ebay and countless retailers have all developed computer hardware, software, payment systems, online stores, and delivery systems which have made the internet the largest center for commercial transactions in history.

Each one of them is absolutely necessary in the success of child pornography. Specifically, Webcam Pornography, having emerged in just last the few years, is a significant part of this illicit industry. This new and growing business induces young people to perform live sex acts in front of their computer-based video cameras while being viewed by paying customers.

You probably know about online chatrooms, internet-based forums where people can speak to each other in real-time (live) with total anonymity. You might also think that chatrooms are often used by predators to solicit children online. Think again. The technology and culture of the internet changes more rapidly than most people realize. Chatrooms are no longer necessary. There are far more efficient ways of finding children to abuse. A predator can reach individual children through perfectly legitimate communications programs from Internet Service Providers (ISP) like AOL and Yahoo.

These easy programs are not only used for direct, private conversations between predators and children, but for the transmission of illegal video images as well. In these instances, young people are supplying live pornographic images of themselves, at the direction of the predator who can instruct them exactly what to do on camera. These services are established very simply by children online without supplying identification or proof of either age or parental consent.

Often a child will begin by exposing their body in front of a web camera, mounted on their computer, in the privacy of their own room. Using the easily accessed technology of online webcasting, the camera sends the images of the young person anywhere in the world to a specific person who is watching the live images from their computer. The predator can type instructions or speak to the child over the internet, telling them exactly what to do for their remote pleasure.

Why would a child do such a thing? Those who become involved are not limited to one socio-demographic group. They are from wealthy, middle-class and poor families. They are children who are honors students and those struggling with their grades. They are children of divorce and with stable, traditional families. Often, though, these minors feel empowered and emboldened by meeting people online and in person through their secret web relationships. They also feel safe. They are usually alone, in their own home, away from the world.

While the answer of voluntary involvement is complex, it also involves money. This is where unwilling corporations become an integral part of the transaction. A predator can arrange to pay the child directly with cash using Paypal or any other online payment system. It is very easy to make an anonymous payment and very easy for the child to receive the money. However, predators are usually very savvy to what children are looking for. They know that young people do not necessarily want money, but the things money can get them. That's where "Wish Lists" come in; a wonderful convenience for gift-giving. Wish Lists are specifically chosen items that young people want from certain online retailers. They work much like a Bridal Registry. Anyone can go to a web-based catalog and register the items they wish to have. Their items are stored for anyone to access.

It is a wonderful tool for marketers when friends and family want to send gifts to loved ones. The shopper simply goes to the child's Wish List and selects an item the child has personally listed as a gift they would like to receive. It makes birthdays, graduations, and holidays very easy for anyone looking to buy a present for someone they know.

It has also become a mechanism for seducing children; making it very easy for predators to tempt young people into exhibiting sexual acts online. For the willing minor, it is very easy. Create a Wish List at your favorite online store. Then tell the person contacting you that you will perform certain acts for specific items on the list. Predators are more than willing to comply. The child simply performs the acts and the gifts begin arriving at their door.

* * *

"By removing my shirt, I had signaled that I could be manipulated. More gifts and money arrived, along with increasingly explicit requests. They wanted me to take off my pants, remove my underwear, and eventually masturbate on camera. The seduction was slow; each new request went only a bit further than the last, and the horror of what was happening did not strike me at the time. I wish I could say that I hated what was happening. Perhaps that would absolve some of my sense of guilt. But the truth is, I did not. As more clothes came off, more people contacted me. The compliments were endless, the gifts and payments terrific. I thought I had achieved online what eluded me in real life: I was popular."

Justin Berry
Testimony before U.S. House of Representatives

* * *

While the child is, at first, not physically abused, it remains a profound molestation of their character, dignity and self-worth. Further, once the images are uploaded to the predator, they can be recorded and posted on the world wide web for years. Thousands of other children have become unknowing participants in the online pornography industry. These minors have been tricked into stripping and masturbating online for what they believe is a single viewer. These performances are placed on commercial pornography sites without the knowledge or consent of the minor. There are people who make their living searching the internet for children with webcams, luring them into sexual performances and selling the resulting pornographic videos. "Here, a single child is being fed upon by hundreds of predators, all in direct, daily contact. Numerous listings of children, including sites such as MySpace.com and BuddyPick.com are now the favored sites, the virtual Sears catalogue for pedophiles," reported Kurt Eichenwald after a six month investigation by *The New York Times*. "Each year, each week, each day the predators are becoming more sophisticated with computers, facilitating the growth and evolution of child pornography. It is why this business is exploding," he concludes.

In the most tragic cases, young people will often agree to meet their regular online "dates" in person. These meetings often end in horrible cases of rape, kidnapping and murder.

* * *

"No one wants to believe that predators abuse and torture children and sell or swap the pictures of that abuse. We do not like to think that even though our children have been warned about strangers, children are still logging onto the internet and meeting strangers, child predators and pedophiles. It is because this problem is so horrific that we need to know more about it. Our nation's parents, children and educators need to know exactly what dangers are lurking on the internet. They need to appreciate how serious this problem is so that they can prepare their children for what, or who, is waiting for them online."

U.S. Congressman Joe Barton, Texas

While adult pornography has some First Amendment freedom of expression protections, there are no such protections for child pornography. Within United States law, any images, real or simulated, showing a child in a sex act is illegal. For images that do not involve a child engaged in a sex act, a court must find that it entails "lascivious exhibition of the genitals or pubic area" of a minor to determine that it is child pornography. As a result, courts have ruled that images of naked children were not automatically pornographic, and thus not illegal. At first glance, this may sound shortsighted, but consider a parent's right to take innocent photos of their children laughing and playing during bath time. The courts also held that the mere presence of clothing on a photographed child was not, in itself, adequate to declare the image lawful.

Instead, courts often apply a six-pronged test, developed in the 1986 case, *United States vs. Dost*, to determine whether an image meets the "lascivious exhibition" standard. While one standard is nudity, the test also requires a court to examine the child's pose and attire, the suggestiveness and intent of the image along with other factors. However, no single standard under the Dost case is absolute, so courts must continuously examine potentially illegal images while considering each part of the test.

No matter how laws are interpreted in the United States, suppliers of child pornography can operate outside of the law anywhere in the world. For those savvy enough, the internet offers total anonymity. Anyone, anywhere at any time can take control of a child, exploit them in front of a camera and offer their abuse for sale online. It is absolutely no different from other forms of child trafficking, just broader in its exposure of the child. Justin Berry, who began appearing naked online when he was thirteen, testified before the U.S. House of Representatives in April, 2006. There he told the Congress, "The law enforcement effort is no match for them. Until recently, I never understood why these child predators always laughed about the government. Now I know the child predators are at least partially right. They have little to fear from law enforcement. Based on my case, efforts to prosecute these people are riddled with mistakes and bureaucracy. Unless something changes, hundreds, or even thousands, of children will be lost forever."

* * *

The scope of the danger facing our children via the internet is immense. By all accounts, at any given time, thousands of predators are on the internet prowling for children. The explosive increase in child pornography fueled by the internet is evidenced by the fact that from 1998 to 2004, the National Center for Missing & Exploited Children's Cyber Tipline experienced a thirty-fold increase in the number of child pornography reports.

The challenge we face in cyberspace was recently underscored by a new national survey, released in August 2006, conducted by University of New Hampshire researchers for the National Center for Missing & Exploited Children. The study revealed that one third of all children aged ten to seventeen who used the internet were exposed to unwanted sexual material. Much of it was extremely graphic.

Because it can invade our lives more deeply than any other form of child exploitation, our disdain for the topic of child pornography cannot allow us to avoid going to any lengths to protect and save the children involved.

Beyond properly equipping United States Federal law enforcement to effectively investigate and prosecute both pornographers and predators, we must, as a nation, take the necessary steps to eradicate this abuse of children everywhere in the world. Since the United States brings economic sanctions against countries that commit human rights violations, "why should we sit idly by when child pornographers operate with the clear complicity of their governments overseas?" asks Andrew Vachss, an author and attorney specializing in the protection of children. Specific action must be taken swiftly. According to Vachss, "When a U.S. investigation reveals an overseas component to a child pornography ring, our government must demand full access to all available evidence and insist that the host country will prosecute all offenders and enforce appropriate penalties."

Child pornographers are counting on our unwillingness to face the ugly realities of what they are doing, thereby allowing them to continue. Only their predatory customers need to know the truth for their businesses to succeed. These criminals and sexual parasites desperately want us to ignore what is being offered through our home computers, what our children may be enticed to do and what is happening to exploited children all over the world who have no choice.

We do not have to comply.

Much more is needed for us to fight for the young people who cannot fight for themselves. Whether they are being held captive by child traffickers or alone in their bedrooms, they need to be rescued. To save them from a fate worse than anyone can envision, we must call for more trained investigators and more computer experts on the side of law enforcement utilizing the most advanced computer equipment. Legally, the federal government must have the ability to force cooperation from other governments.

Because of the huge profits it generates, the perpetrators of these crimes have far more financial resources at their disposal than the dedicated people fighting them. Very simply, these children are worth are great deal of money to pornographers and worldwide criminal syndicates.

What are they worth to us?

* * *

Masha, often referred to as the "internet Porn Girl" had appeared in over 200 sexually explicit images that remain in circulation on the web. As new photos continued to appear, authorities began a desperate worldwide search for her. They took the unusual step of digitally removing her body from the photos. Then they released the images of what appeared to be a hotel room to the international media, hoping that someone would identify the setting. Very quickly they learned where they had been taken: Disney World. Yet, the girl's identity remained unknown.

Several months later the hunt ended when a search through child pornography photo databases found a match. The girl, only eight years old at the time the photographs were taken, was a Russian orphan, adopted in 1998 by Matthew Mancuso. A retired engineer from Plum, Pennsylvania, he had adopted Masha for the express purpose of molesting her and using her to produce pornographic photos. When federal agents raided his home, they found computer disks filled with child pornography.

They also found Masha. After five years of hidden abuse, shared with the world, her first words to the agents were, "Is this about my secret?"

* * *

Eight

I am Tiri

The Price of a Tank of Gas

* * *

When Tiri wakes, it is about noon. The moment she opens her eyes, she knows exactly who and what she has become. The soreness in her genitals reminds her of the thirteen men she had sex with the night before. Tiri is fifteen years old. Sold by her parents a year ago to a woman broker from a Northern village, the broker assured her parents they would be well paid for their daughter. After some negotiation, they received $1,318 for Tiri. Now, Tiri's resistance and desire to escape the brothel are breaking down, and acceptance and resignation are taking their place. After she was sold and taken to the brothel, she discovered that the work was not what she thought it would be. Tiri had a sheltered childhood and was ignorant of what it meant to work in a brothel. Her first client hurt her and at the earliest opportunity, she ran away. On the street with no money, she was quickly caught, dragged back, beaten, and raped. That night she was forced to take on a chain of clients until the early morning. The beatings and work continued night after night until her will was broken. Now she is sure that she is a bad person.

Source: Free The Slaves

* * *

A child is not a tourist attraction. Unless the child is located in Tijuana, Bangkok, Cambodia, India, Greece, or thousands of other *child sex tourism* locations across the world. They are children born into poverty and sold for sex. And while the thousands of men who flock to these destinations each year, many of them Americans, may think that they're involved in nothing more than prostitution, by any definition it is rape.

Since the 1960s and the introduction of jet travel to the general population, international travel has increased nearly ten-fold. This has opened the world to travelers as they discover distant lands, cultures, and traditions. The people of developing countries have welcomed the expansion of the international tourism industry as a much-needed source of income, sometimes the largest source, within their own nations.

Of course, not all travelers are seeking to meet new people or explore the magnificent wonders of the world. Some are traveling simply to purchase sex with children. "It's the worst kind of human exploitation imaginable. Can you imagine young children ...being used as sexual slaves for predators? It is a sin against humanity, and it is a horrendous crime," asks former Secretary of State Colin Powell.

Sex tourism is a lucrative global industry. The International Labor Organization reported that ten to fifteen percent of the gross domestic product of Indonesia, Malaysia, the Philippines, and Thailand derives from sex tourism. And while these countries have been popular destinations for child sex tourism for many years, Mexico and Central America have become popular destinations since the late 1990s as perpetrators in those markets traffic children into the trade.

Child sex promoters invite people to travel from their own country to another in order to engage in commercial sex acts with children, thereby avoiding exposure and legal retribution for the customers. Instead of risking highly publicized sting operations in the United States, American men surf the internet looking for the opportunity to have sex with very young girls and boys in other countries, far away from the law and cameras of network television news.

They find their best opportunities in developing countries which offer complete anonymity and the ready availability of children in prostitution. The crime is typically fueled by weak law enforcement, corruption, the internet, ease of travel, and poverty. The "tourists" are motivated only by their incomprehensible lust for children and come from all ethnic and socio-economic backgrounds.

Child sex tourists are typically males from nations in Western European nations, North America, Asia and the Middle East. There are some preferences in destinations among child sex tourists. For example, those from Japan usually travel to Thailand, while Americans tend to travel to Mexico or Central America. In Cambodia, a virtual haven for child sex tourists, it is estimated that one-third of the prostitutes are children, according to studies conducted by ECPAT. Mu Soc Hua, Cambodia's Minister of Women's Affairs, says the number of children involved in Cambodian prostitution is "around 30,000."

Finally, studies from the U.S. State Department and the International Labor Organization conclude that Americans account for twenty-five percent of child sex tourists worldwide. That number is closer to eighty percent for destinations which are closer in proximity to the United States like Mexico and Costa Rica.

Some people do not intend to have sex with young people when they travel abroad looking for prostitutes, but they take advantage of children sexually once they arrive. Others travel specifically for the purpose of exploiting children. The difference in original intent, however, has no relevance to the child being abused. The damage is done.

Whatever the intent of the perpetrator, there is almost always a rationalization for their sexual encounters with children. In attempting to justify their actions, they often have the idea that they are helping the youngsters to financially better themselves and their families. "Paying a child for his or her services allows a tourist to avoid guilt by convincing himself he is helping the child and the child's family to escape economic hardship," explains John Miller of the U.S. State Department. Others justify what they are doing with the belief that children in other countries are less inhibited and open to sexuality at an earlier age. They rationalize that their destination country does not have the same social taboos against having sex with children.

Still other perpetrators are drawn towards child sex while abroad because they enjoy the anonymity that comes with being in a foreign land.

This anonymity provides the child sex tourist with freedom from the moral restraints that would normally govern behavior in his home country. Consequently, some tourists feel that they can discard their moral values when traveling and avoid accountability for their behavior and its consequences. Finally, some sex tourists are fueled by racism and view the welfare of children of third world countries as unimportant.

Beyond the ease of international travel, other factors have led to the rise in child sex tourism. Using the internet, promoters provide potential child sex tourists with pornographic accounts written by other child sex tourists. These clandestine websites offer blogs which detail sexual exploits with children. They also provide information on commercial sex establishments and prices in various destinations around the world, including information on how to find child prostitutes. One website promised nights of sex "with two young Thai girls for the price of a tank of gas." From the safety and anonymity of their homes child sex abusers can make all the necessary arrangements for their trip.

Also, foreign governments may encourage child sex tourism. Some countries have become increasingly tourist-friendly in their search for profitable sources of income. These poverty-stricken governments will often ignore or deny the sex tourism industry within their borders, allowing the industry to abuse children in order to encourage all tourism in their country. Consequently, "efforts to combat child sexual exploitation often run into conflict with foreign governments' efforts to promote the international tourism industry," according to Sowmia Nair, an agent with U.S. State Department. "Police corruption is common. In Thailand and the Philippines, police have been known to guard brothels and even procure children for prostitution. Some police in destination countries directly exploit children themselves."

* * *

"These sluts are so naive. If you promise to marry them and take them along with you to Brussels they do whatever you ask."

Philippe Servaty
Chief Economics Correspondent, *Le Soir*

* * *

Philippe Servaty, a newspaper columnist for *Le Soir*, Brussels' most influential newspaper, traveled to Morocco several times for vacation. While there he persuaded dozens of young girls to pose in front of his camera by promising to marry them and bring them to Belgium with him. Returning home alone, he posted photos online to show other sex tourists what they too could find in Morocco. Unfortunately, when his explicit photos were discovered in Morocco, many of the women were arrested, had their lives ruined, committed suicide or simply disappeared.

One of the girls in the photos, Ramaria, was recognized online by a family member, who beat her up and threw her out of the house. Ramaria went to the police to file a complaint against Servaty, but to pose for pornographic pictures is a crime in Morocco and she was immediately arrested. A Moroccan judge sentenced her to a heavy fine and a prison sentence of one year. Her family cast her out and all her friends abandoned her, while the police began a search for Servaty's other models for prosecution. Thirteen were convicted and sentenced to prison, two attempted suicide and some, the girls police cannot find, are thought to have been murdered by their disgraced families.

When Moroccan police asked Brussels police to arrest Servaty, they simply responded that was not possible. According to Belgian law, he had not done anything wrong.

* * *

"I've been living away from home for three years, working as a dancer in a club. I had many problems because my dad drank a lot. He is very machista, tough. When I was small, he used to hit my mother and that made me mad."

Fernando, 13, Acapulco, Mexico
Source: UNICEF

* * *

Ambassador John Miller has called child-sex tourism "a particularly noxious form of human trafficking." Pope Benedict XVI warned a meeting of Bishops that "no effort must be spared to encourage civil authorities and the international community to fight child abuse and assure young people the necessary legal protection." Colin Powell asks, "Can you imagine the spread of disease that is taking place with this kind of activity? Can you imagine what will happen to these girls when they're fifteen or twenty? What will become of them? They'll have no education. They will have been used and tossed away and ruined. If we allow our citizens to go over and fuel that trade, by their presence and by their money and by their rotten exploitation of these children, we wouldn't be living up to our values if we didn't do something about it."

While it is a moral outrage, child sex tourism is common and widespread in Acapulco, Mexico, where the vast majority of customers are American. Like most sex tourism hotspots in the world, it mostly involves girls. But, in the area from la Condesa to la Diana, there is a group of about 40 boys between the ages of thirteen and sixteen who service American men on vacation. "I give shows in two gay bars," says Fernando, a young male victim. "Sometimes the bar owners invite you to do a special show for a client and they give you 10 pesos for each drink the client has. Many clients want something more, but if you go with someone who's very drunk, you run a risk because they can give you a bad time."

Fernando's story is typical of young girls and boys involved in sex tourism. In poverty, in resorts, in cities and in villages, they are threatened, beaten, mugged, and abused from every angle of their desperate lives. Their existence is one of fear because every adult with whom they come in contact wants something from them. And the children already know, at a very young age, that if they do not provide what is wanted, it will be, as Fernando says, "a bad time."

"The police treat you badly all the time," Fernando continues. "They say you're drugged, that you sell drugs. They have even stripped me to get my money off me. They beat me and my friends if we don't give them their 50 pesos. They told us that if we said anything, they'd kill us."

Acapulco has more than 500 registered clubs and bars offering sexual services. But there are even more unregistered clubs and bars offering access to the sexual services of children. Instead of trying to stop this illegal exploitation, some policemen demand their share of the children's earnings.

There is one other thing that children who serve sex tourists have in common: *They dream.* "I have many foreign friends," Fernando says, "from Switzerland, America, Canada. They send me messages by e-mail. I'd like to learn English and French and be a tourist guide for my friends. It feels good when someone is really concerned about you."

As a child, your parents would tuck you in at night. They would tell you bedtime stories, touch your face, kiss you goodnight and wish you "*sweet dreams*."

What dreams could these children possibly have? Alone in a wilderness of pain, each one is merely a sexual commodity; a disposable source of profit for their owners and pleasure for their customers; just another tourist attraction. On their way home, the men sit on airplanes, laughing and bragging about how easy it was.

And for the price of a tank of gas, they stole the dreams of an innocent child.

* * *

Nine

I am Kalami

I Was a Soldier

* * *

"The battle lasted forever. We were told to kill people by forcing them to stay in their homes while we burned them down. We even had to bury some people alive. One day my friends and I were forced by our commanders to kill a family, to cut up their bodies and to eat them. After this battle, I decided I had to flee and I ran away into the forest. But in Lubero some soldiers found me and brought me back to a military camp. They imprisoned me and beat me every day. Seeing that I was close to death, a soldier decided to send me to the hospital in Lubero, where UN staff found me and demobilized me. Today, I am afraid. I don't know how to read, I don't know where my family is, I have no future. My life is lost. I have nothing to live for. At night I can no longer sleep. I keep thinking of those horrible things I have seen and done when I was a soldier."

Kalami, 15
Source: Adult Wars, Child Soldiers – UNICEF

* * *

Kalami was recruited when he was nine. When Amnesty International delegates met him in Goma, a city in the Democratic Republic of Congo, he was fifteen years old and had spent six years of his life fighting as a *child soldier.*

Armed conflicts pervade human history and our world today as increasing numbers of children are exposed to the brutalities of war. In several countries, boys and girls, some as young as eight, are forcibly used as child soldiers by armed forces and rebel groups. Susceptible because of their age, poverty and lack of education, children are recruited by manipulation, force or threats. Often abducted at school, on the streets or at home, they are inadequately trained, treated harshly, and rapidly pushed into combat. Once forced into service, they are used in battle, for sexual purposes, as spies, or to clear landmines.

"The very concept of the child soldier is an oxymoron; it's a paradox because we look at children as innocent, vulnerable, and needing protection," explains Dr. Alcinda Manuel Honwana, of the Department of Social Anthropology at the University of Cape Town. Yet, with new weapons that are lightweight and easy to fire, children can be taught to unleash deadly force with less training than ever before. Consequently, they are exposed to extreme dangers and horrible suffering, both psychological and physical. Many children have committed acts of unimaginable violence, often against their own families. These acts amount to nothing less than war crimes, which they are unable to comprehend. And while most child soldiers are boys, many girl soldiers are forced to perform sex acts as well as fight in battle.

The current use of children as soldiers has been universally condemned as abhorrent and unacceptable by every valid government and international human rights organization. Yet, throughout history children have fought and died in conflicts around the world, sacrificing their lives for wars they could never understand.

The earliest mentions of minors being involved in wars are found in antiquity. It was customary for youths in the cultures of the Mediterranean basin to serve as aides, charioteers and armor bearers to adult warriors. Examples of this practice are recorded in David's service to King Saul in the Bible, the story of Hercules and Hylas from Greek mythology, Egyptian art, as well as ancient philosophy and literature. In ancient Greece the practice of children in war was formalized as part of a young man's educational training whereby man-boy partnerships were considered to make an especially effective fighting force. Later, in Europe, children were routinely taken on campaigns of war, together with the rest of a military man's family, as part of the baggage. Though children were kept at the rear of the battlegrounds, they were exposed to extreme danger including harm from rearguard attacks. This is exactly what happened at the battle of Agincourt where the children of the English army were massacred by the French.

The Children's Crusade in 1212 recruited thousands of children as untrained soldiers under the assumption that divine power would enable them to conquer the enemy. Although none of the children entered combat, their exposure allowed them to be captured and sold into slavery.

During the age of sail, young boys served on the crews of British Royal Navy ships. You may have seen them depicted in the powerful movie, *Master and Commander* with Russell Crowe. These children, called *Powder Monkeys*, were responsible for many important tasks including bringing powder and shot from the ship's magazine to the guns during battle.

Through a law signed by Nicholas I of Russia in 1827, a disproportionate number of Jewish boys, known as the *cantonists*, were forced into military training establishments to serve in the army. The 25-year conscription term officially commenced at the age of 18, but boys as young as eight were routinely taken to fulfill the hard quota.

In World War II, children frequently participated in popular insurrections like the Warsaw Uprising of 1944 and other anti-fascist resistance movements across Nazi-occupied Europe.

On the opposite side of the war, the Hitler Youth movement was an official organization in Nazi Germany that trained young people physically while indoctrinating them with Nazi ideology. By the end of the Second World War, members were taken into the army at an increasingly younger age. During the Battle of Berlin in 1945, children were a major part of the German defenses simply because there was no one left to fight. These remaining children are depicted in the well known photographs of

Hitler's last public appearance on April 20, 1945. That day, his 56th birthday, Hitler awarded the Iron Cross to several Hitler Youth, no more than twelve years old, outside his bunker where he died a few days later.

* * *

"He ordered us to loot everything they had, to drive them away and to destroy their homes. The population responded and tried to stop us, and so our commander gave the order to kill anyone who put up any resistance. He ordered me personally to do that and told two other soldiers to watch over me and kill me if I refused to obey. And so I killed, I fired on these people. They brought me a woman and her children and I had to put them in a hole and bury them alive. They were screaming and pleading with me to spare them and release them. I took pity on them, but then I looked over my shoulder at the two soldiers watching me, and I said to myself: 'If I let them go, these soldiers are going to kill me.' And so I went ahead and buried the woman and children alive, to save my own life."

Arsene, 13
Source: UNICEF

* * *

Today, child soldiering is very different. Contrary to the efforts of several international organizations, large numbers of children continue to be exploited in war and placed in the line of fire.

Serving as slaves with no value, young children are coerced into fighting and dying in atrocities fueled by tribal and idealogic hatred and ignorance; conscripted into armed conflicts, serving in government armies, armed militias, and rebel groups. Some children are kidnapped and forced to serve while others are threatened personally or made to fight in order to avoid violence against their families. Desperate from warfare and poverty, some even cling to false promises of compensation. Children involved in armed conflict are "frequently killed or injured during combat or while carrying out other tasks," explains Victoria Forbes Adams, Director of the Coalition to Stop the Use of Child Soldiers. "They are forced to engage in hazardous activities such as laying mines or explosives. Child soldiers are usually forced to live under harsh conditions with insufficient food and little or no access to healthcare. They are almost always treated brutally, subjected to beatings and humiliating treatment. Punishments for mistakes or desertion are often very severe. Girl soldiers are particularly at risk of rape, sexual harassment and abuse as well as being involved in combat," she explains.

Fabienne was thirteen when she was abducted in Burundi by combatants whom she believed were members of an armed opposition group. "I don't know how many people had sex with me. A man would come, then another and another. You couldn't refuse, they said they'd kill you if you ran away," she explained to representatives of Amnesty International.

According to an ongoing research project of the United Nations, child soldiers are a global phenomenon, but the problem is especially critical in Africa, Asia, Middle East, and Eurasia. In 2006 they estimated the worldwide number of child soldiers at 250,000 to 300,000, a third of whom were girls, in more than 30 countries. However, they report it is difficult to know the correct number, as most of them are deployed in secretive rebel groups. More than two million children are estimated to have died as a direct result of armed conflict during the period of 1995–2005. During that time at least six million children have been seriously injured or permanently disabled. Further, between 8,000 and 10,000 children are killed or maimed by landmines each year.

Child soldiering is "a unique and severe manifestation of trafficking in persons," according to the U.S. State Department. Often hoping for food, clothing, and shelter, a child's decision to join an armed group is never considered to be a free choice. Many are seeking only to survive and are often forced to use alcohol or narcotics as a way to reduce their fear in battle, desensitize them to violence or enhance their endurance and performance.

* * *

"After capturing a village what happened is that they would give us chanvre (cannabis) and force us to kill people to toughen us up. Sometimes they brought us women and girls to rape. The commanding officers didn't justify why they did that. Every time they

captured somewhere, they would get the kadogos (child soldier) to do these things in front of the adult soldiers, as if it was a show, in order to humiliate the people of the village. The scene held no interest for us, but they would beat us if we refused. The unlucky ones were shot and would die. They killed kadogos like that when they refused to obey."

Albert, 14
Source: Amnesty International

* * *

It seems hard to imagine why or how anyone could use a child to fight wars. Yet, children are recruited "because they are perceived as cheap and expendable, easily brutalized into fearless killing and unquestioning obedience. Child soldiers are often chosen for the most dangerous assignments or forced to participate in appalling human rights abuses," declares Larry Cox, Executive Director of Amnesty International USA.

These are some of the actions forced on Child Soldiers:

Protect locations as human shields. Placing a school, orphanage or hospital near military targets is often viewed as a legitimate defense against attack.

Commit suicide missions and bombings. Children, especially children of the enemy, are considered expendable. Many times their only purpose is to deliver one bomb or grenade to a target. If they are stopped or killed, there is an endless supply of children who can be forced to try again.

Commit atrocities against their families or communities in order to subdue the remainder of the population. Often children are used to win wars by destroying family and communal ties. Armies who use children understand that they have a unique and powerful weapon. Consider a band of ten men entering a village of 100 people. They are outnumbered, but must take the village and completely subdue the population. At gunpoint they kidnap a few boys from the village and force them to torture, rape and kill their families. Once a community sees a few of its families murdered by their own children, the battle is over. It places a terror so fierce in the hearts of people that they can do nothing but submit to the enemy soldiers.

Lay mine fields. Burying mines, while simple, is extremely dangerous. Children are used in order to spare the lives of adult troops.

Clear mine fields. Using their bodies and lives to find and explode hidden mines, children are sent into known minefields. They are meant to locate and clear mines by triggering them under their feet. Having been killed by the explosion, the next child is sent in, and the next, and the next. The process continues until a safe passageway has been determined.

Provide an expendable target. Children are sent into enemy lines in order to draw fire from the opposition. When shots are fired at the children, this exposes the enemy's position.

Replenish diminished ranks. After prolonged conflicts there are fewer and fewer adults left to fight. Recruiting ages always decrease after years of war.

Commit sabotage. Because people still believe children are harmless and innocent, they are often able to gain access to places where adults would raise suspicion.

The most important reason that armed groups or even some governments recruit children as soldiers is their diminished capability to distinguish between right and wrong, as well as between hard reality and just an adventurous game. Up to a certain age, children do not have a full grasp of the finality of death and the severity of killing a human being. They lack the ability to correctly identify dangers and to assess the risks of specific situations. In other words, they can be programmed to do anything to anybody. Given the proper training, their behavior can be robotic. Children are malleable; easy to influence and can be made to follow a specific cause with cultish loyalty. Commanding officers who have seen battle will attest to the fact that when mounting a deadly assault, the best soldiers to have are trained killers with guns who follow orders without question. Often, because their young minds are programmed by their superiors with severe behavior modification techniques, fostering utter devotion and clarity, children can be the most deadly and ruthless of combatants.

* * *

"I feel so bad about the things that I did. It disturbs me so much that I inflicted death on other people," explains Mary, a fifteen-year-old former child soldier who was forced to join

an armed rebel group in central Africa. "When I go home I must do some traditional rites because I have killed. I must perform these rites and cleanse myself. I still dream about the boy from my village whom I killed. I see him in my dreams, and he is talking to me, saying I killed him for nothing, and I am crying." Through tears she pleads, "I would like you to give a message. Please do your best to tell the world what is happening to us, the children. So that other children don't have to pass through this violence."

Source: U.S. State Department

* * *

Mary was forcibly abducted at night from her home by the Lord's Resistance Army, an armed opposition movement fighting the government in Uganda. After thirty-five days of perfunctory military training she was sent into service and made to kill a boy who tried to escape. She saw another boy being hacked to death for not raising the alarm when a friend ran away. She was beaten when she dropped a water container and ran for cover under gunfire.

Her plea is to all of us.

"The horrifying reality of killings, torture, rape and sexual slavery endured by tens of thousands of child soldiers in conflicts across the continent must be ended," Larry Cox tells us. Child soldiers are killed and wounded at far higher rates than adults. Survivors suffer a myriad of traumas and psychological problems from the violence and brutality they experienced and, sometimes, perpetrated. Their development as an individual capable of a normal, healthy life is irreparably damaged. Often, their families and hometowns reject former child soldiers because of the violence they or their group inflicted on the community.

When other children their age are in Middle School, they are hardened soldiers, veterans of the most vicious warfare on earth. They were empty vessels into which the worst of humanity poured violence, terror and hate. Now, after all they have been through, no one wants them and there is nowhere for them to go.

* * *

"*I was living in my village with my mother and my brothers and sisters. One day, our village was attacked by the mayi-mayi. The mayi-mayi soldiers stole everything we had. A few days later, our village was attacked again by the* RCD-*Goma, who accused us of collaboration with the mayi-mayi and of giving them food. I watched as soldiers killed many of my relatives in the village and raped my two sisters and my mother. I was hiding but I saw how many soldiers raped my sisters and my mother. I was scared, and I thought that if I joined the army, I would be protected. I wanted to defend myself. Once in the army I was trained to carry and use a fire arm and I performed guard duty night and days. It was horrible because I was only twelve years old, but I was frequently beaten and raped during the night by the other soldiers. One day, a commander wanted me to become his wife, so I tried to escape. They caught me, whipped me and raped me every night for many days. When I was just fourteen, I had a baby. I don't even know who his father is. I ran away again and this time I managed to escape. But today I have nowhere to go and no food to give to the baby, and I am afraid to go home, because I was a soldier.*"

Natalia, 16
Source: Amnesty International

* * *

Ten

I am Andrei

Spare Parts

* * *

"I wanted to buy a house and a new car and some clothes. It was my dream. I wanted to leave him at the orphanage, but my mother was insisting that we could get $70,000 for organs." Police in Russian discovered a grandmother trying to sell her five-year-old grandson for his organs. Five-year-old Andrei was sold for $90,000 in an operation that stunned police in Ryazan, an hour's drive south of Moscow. While illegal adoptions are nothing new in Russia, police were alarmed that those suspected of selling Andrei, who had been living at an orphanage, were his own grandmother and an uncle. They were also shocked that he was bought for such a high price because he was sold for his organs; kidneys, eyes, possibly the heart or the lungs. A police detective said, "Such a betrayal. But there is an illegal market for organs, especially children's organs." Police said Andrei's grandmother Nina not only sold her grandson, she lied to her own son about the price, pocketing $20,000. Russian police will not reveal who the prospective buyers of the child were, or who the buyers are in other cases, only that the buyers in this and other cases are generally "westerners."

Andrei is back at the orphanage, where attendants say, he misses his grandmother.

Source: CNN

* * *

A nightmarish concept, *organ harvesting* is another growing reality of child trafficking. "Labor is sold, sex is sold, sperm and ova are sold, even babies are sold in international adoption. What makes kidneys so special, so exempt?" asks Dr. Abdullah Daar, Director of the Program in Applied Ethics and Biotechnology at the University of Toronto.

Every day medical science advances our ability to save and improve lives by using body parts from other humans. Since the early 1970s, when drugs were developed to control the body's rejection of foreign objects, organ transplantation has developed from being an experimental procedure performed in a few advanced medical centers, to a fairly common operation performed in hospitals and clinics throughout the world.

For example, kidney transplantation, the most common transplant procedure, is now conducted in the U.S., most European and Asian countries, several South American and Middle Eastern countries, and four African nations.

Unfortunately, the rapid spread of transplant capabilities has created a global scarcity of transplantable human organs.

Certainly, there is no shortness of sick people in need of a new organ or limb. With each new medical discovery or advance, hope is born in the lives of people suffering from illnesses previously considered terminal. Consequently, there is a very long and growing waiting list for everything from livers, hearts, kidneys, corneas, bone marrow, and anything else that can be replaced.

In the United States, organ transplants are strictly regulated by a complex congressionally mandated priority system that places patients on waiting list for years. According to the United Network for Organ Sharing, as of September 15, 2006, there were 92,902 people waiting for organ donations just in the United States where, in 2005, 6,124, approximately seventeen a day, died waiting for an organ.

It is simply a matter of supply and demand. Where there is a huge demand and very short supply, not only do prices increase, but so does crime.

Imagine looking at the market for human body parts from a completely inhuman perspective. Is there really a shortage? There are approximately seven billion people in the world. That is seven billion human factories potentially producing body parts for those who need them.

From the point of view of organized crime, there is no supply problem. This only presents the problems of acquisition and distribution. However, if they are already operating in the trade of young human flesh for sex and other uses, why not offer these children for sale one body part at a time? After all, if they are in your possession and control, you can certainly move them to wherever their organs are needed, run blood tests to screen for matching blood types and illness. In other words, you can accommodate any customer willing to pay the price.

"A kind of *body mafia* is involved," explains Nancy Scheper-Hughes, an anthropologist and Director of Organ Watch, an organization dedicated to investigating every aspect of the trade in human organs. She says this franchise of transnational crime is "a new triangle of slavery, which unites the desperate patient in Israel, with organ brokers in Turkey, and doctors in Turkey and Israel with paid organ donors from Eastern Europe, Romania, Moldova and Russia as well. This is often done with the criminal backing of brokers who are also involved in brokering women's bodies for prostitution, children for international adoptions and small arms. It's literally a criminal network."

* * *

The *United Nations Convention Against Transnational Organized Crime*, which covers prevention, enforcement and sanctions in trafficking of humans, includes in its definition of human exploitation, the illegal extraction and selling of organs.

The World Health Organization has also condemned the practice of selling human body parts, prohibiting the advertisement of organs in exchange for money, and established the principle of equality in terms of human organ donations.

In fact, human organ sales are illegal in most of the world. But, the legal sanctions in one country can quickly stimulate trafficking in a neighboring country. Wealthy patients are very willing and able to travel even great distances to obtain a transplant. Assisting in this process is the anonymity and global reach of the internet, allowing traffickers to successfully market their warehouse of spare parts for humans. Doctors and patients of all nationalities are seeking body parts from wherever they can get them and the internet is the perfect resource for this new illegal distribution network.

One example was uncovered by journalists and broken up by police in the mid-1990s. For years very wealthy citizens of Japan used intermediaries with connections to organized crime in order to locate paid kidney donors in other countries. One ring of Yakuza gangsters operated through connections at a major medical center in Boston.

One of the serious problems with illegal trafficking of human organs is that it circumvents all screening and testing procedures set up and maintained to ensure recipients will not receive diseased or otherwise contaminated tissue or organs. "At some point, you cannot turn over every rock looking for trouble," said Dr. Ian Tellis, a renal transplant surgeon at Montefiore Medical Center in the Bronx. "We are obligated not to facilitate something terrible, but if the circumstances seem reasonable we go ahead."

The gap between supply and demand is wider in countries where there are strong religious or cultural sanctions with respect to the handling of a dead body. In the Middle East, for instance, transplantable cadaver organs are extremely scarce owing to the elaborate religious protocol for the proper treatment and burial of the dead in both Jewish and Muslim customs.

The consequence is that sanctions in one country stimulate organ sales in those nearby. Wealthy patients will travel great distances to secure a transplant, even in areas where medical treatment and survival rates are very poor. In India, for example, there is a virtual organs mall operating out of private clinics, especially in Bombay and Madras. Until a new law banning the sale of living donor organs in India was put into affect, wealthy patients from the Gulf States, Kuwait, Saudi Arabia, Oman and the United Arab Emirates, traveled to India to purchase kidneys and other organs. While the law ended the open sale of these organs to desperate foreign patients, the market has been driven underground. Recent reports by human-rights activists, journalists and representatives from Doctors Without Borders state that the open international kidney trade has declined leaving in its wake an even larger underground market controlled and organized by global crime syndicates specializing in human trafficking.

In a careful study conducted by Dr. Carol Allais, Department Chair of Sociology at the University of South Africa, a team of researchers found that since the mid-1980s "organized transplant package tours, or *transplant tourism*, have carried affluent patients from Israel, Saudi Arabia, Oman and Kuwait initially to India for transplant and later to Turkey, Iran and Iraq and, most recently Russia, Romania and Moldova where kidney sellers are recruited, sometimes coercively, from army barracks, prisons, unemployment offices, flea markets, shopping malls and bars."

* * *

"The global shortage of transplantable organs has networks of organized crime – the body mafia – giving rise to ambulatory organ buyers, itinerant kidney hunters, outlaw surgeons, medical technicians, makeshift transplant units, and underground laboratories."

Dr. Carol Allais,
University of South Africa

* * *

The market forces of supply and demand are not limited to organized crime. Transplant package tours are arranged in Europe, North America and Japan to take transplant patients to China where their surgery is arranged, with the complicity of Chinese doctors and surgeons to coincide with public executions that provide the primary source of lucrative transplant organs. Minutes before their execution, condemned prisoners are surgically prepped for the sole purpose of harvesting of their organs.

Mr. Lin, a recent immigrant from China to San Francisco, is a witness to this practice. Just before leaving China, he visited a friend at a medical center in Shanghai. In the bed next to his friend was a wealthy and politically connected man who stated that he was waiting for a kidney transplant later that day. He explained that his new kidney would arrive as soon as a prisoner was executed that morning. Minutes before the condemned prisoner was shot in the head, doctors present at the execution would quickly extract his kidneys and rush them to the hospital where two transplant-surgery teams would be assembled and waiting. Many other recent Chinese immigrants to the United States relate similar experiences.

"We have patients who have received a kidney in China," said Dr. Mark Hardy, director of Renal Transplantation at Columbia Presbyterian Medical Center. "We take care of them even if they abuse the system. In some cases their decision is not so unreasonable."

Further fueling the world-wide harvest of organs are the ancient practices of cultures which devalue human life for the benefit of tradition and mysticism. In India, a dowry is a gift of money or valuables given by a bride's family to the groom's when they are married. It is regarded as contribution provided by her family to the married household's expenses. Trading a kidney for a dowry has become a common strategy for economically disadvantaged parents in arranging a marriage for their daughters. This has created a situation whereby poor families must give away their kidneys in order to give away their daughters.

In African a mystic practice involves the use of human body parts and vital organs to produce medicine. Certain beliefs state that *Muti* medicine increases the luck and health of the person who consumes it. Muti medicine is prepared by traditional healers known as Sangomas, who dismember their victims while they are still alive in the belief that by doing so, the medicine will be more powerful. Most Muti victims are children because it is believed they have more good luck and health. The dying screams of young children are also believed to make Muti medicine more powerful by waking the spirits and empowering them. And according to Muti traditions and beliefs, the power of a virgin is greater than one who is sexually active. Although most Muti sacrifices occur in South Africa, there are an increasing number of cases in England, Italy, Belgium and Germany.

In early 2006, a Catholic nun at an orphanage in Mozambique reported that their children were disappearing. Investigator Marina Rini of the human rights organization, Terre des Hommes says, "We know that (criminal) gangs offer children for sale dead or alive. We can only conclude that the missing children die or are killed for their organs."

* * *

A wealthy seventy-year-old New York kidney dialysis patient was told that because of his age and other factors he would have to wait as long as twelve years for a kidney even after he had registered at 10 U.S. transplant centers. Instead he found a doctor who arranged for an African donor to come to the United States for an illicit operation that cost more than $100,000. The man's nephrologist "certainly knew what was going on, but the operation could not be done at his hospital in New York, so we had to go out of state, where the doctor would not question too closely," a family member said. "We had to pretend we knew this person, that he was an old friend who was doing this," the relative continued. "I am sorry that our system made this necessary but I am so grateful to see him playing with his grandchildren."

Source: *The New York Daily News*

* * *

Nancy Scheper-Hughes says that the demand for human organs "by the wealthy transplant patients who purchase them, is similar to the parties in the international market in child adoption. Those looking for transplant organs, both surgeons and their patients, are often willing to set aside questions about how the purchased commodity was obtained."

This is a horrible scenario for you to imagine, but what if someone in your family, perhaps your young child, was very sick? What if their life could be saved with a transplant, but no donor was available. If you had the financial resources, if the money was there, would you wait patiently while your child's name slowly worked its way up the list of transplant candidates? How long would you watch someone you love suffer? How long would you let them drift toward death?

Out of frustration, your doctor or someone you know gives you a name to call, perhaps someone in a foreign country. They tell you this person might be able to help. If there was any chance to cure your child, would you consider it? If you had no options left, would you make the call? And if it was suddenly possible for your child to return home healthy, if you had hope again, would you ask where the organs came from? Or would you pay the money and let your child live?

Horrible questions. Hard questions. But, they do bring us closer to understanding what drives this international market for the organs, *spare parts*, sacrificed by children who had no choice.

* * *

Eleven

I am Nazmie

Silent Despair

* * *

"When I was ten my parents arranged for me to marry in the forest. They pretended it was just a party. But it was a wedding and they sent me away. My mother never told me I was going to be married. They came and took me by force. I cried but it didn't make any difference."

Nazime, 10
SOURCE: Foundation for Women's Health
Research & Development

* * *

A girl is promised in marriage to much older man. A dowry has already been paid and her family is pleased to have one less mouth to feed. No matter how old she is, her childhood is over. Forced into constant domestic service, she will no longer be educated. She is expected to get pregnant right away, even at an early age. She is now the property of her husband. With her freedom gone, the course of her life has been set because of *forced child marriage*.

Forced child marriages can occur through coercion, inducements, deception and abduction. However it happens, the result is enslavement. "Forcing children, especially girls, into early marriages, can be physically and emotionally harmful," states Carol Bellamy, former Executive Director of UNICEF. "It violates their rights to personal freedom and growth."

Despite national laws and international agreements prohibiting child marriage, millions of children in developing nations are now married. For example, in 1929 India prohibited child marriage under the *Child Marriage Restraint Act*. However, today in parts of India, nearly eighty percent of the marriages are among girls under the age of fifteen.

"Child marriage is more likely to occur in rural areas. In general, poverty, lack of education, and unemployment are the root causes of social ills associated with early marriage," reports Charlotte Ponticelli, former Senior Coordinator for International Women's Issues Office of the U.S. State Department. Forced child marriage, she says, "is especially troubling in that it treats young girls as property, deprives them of having a voice in determining their own future, and brings their childhood to a premature end. Most tragic, perhaps, are instances of poor families forced to sell their daughters out of economic survival.

The vast majority of young people forced or sold into marriage are girls, primarily caused by cultural attitudes which perceive young females as economic liabilities. Within poor communities, a daughter may be the only commodity a family has left to offer for trade. Their unwanted girls can be used as currency or even to settle debts. This creates the subsequent cause of gender imbalance; a simple shortage of women due to a preference for males. Many cultures within Egypt, Afghanistan, Bangladesh, Ethiopia, Pakistan, India, the Middle East, Africa, South America and others, consider female children nearly worthless, making gender selection through abortion or abandonment a common practice.

In the some of these areas, young girls are rarely allowed to leave their homes unless it is to work or to get married. Without an education or livelihood, these girls are often married by the time they are eleven years old. Some families allow girls who are only seven years old to marry. Among these cultures, it is very unusual for a girl to reach the age of sixteen and not be someone's wife.

In most cases, the forced marriage of young people brings them ongoing problems for the rest of their lives. "When marriage occurs too early and without adequate preparation, the health, education and economic consequences can be negative for both the girl and for the future generations that she bears," says Dr. Geeta Rao Gupta, President of the International Center for Research on Women. According to the United Nations report, *Early Marriage: Child Spouses*, authored by researcher Stephen H. Umemoto, forced child marriages have profound physical, intellectual, psychological and emotional impact, cutting off educational opportunities and chances of personal growth. For girls, the report says, "it will almost certainly mean premature pregnancy and child bearing, and is likely to lead to a life-time of domestic and sexual subservience over which they have no control."

* * *

Fatoumata is not sure how old she was when she was forced to marry her cousin. "At first I ran away and stayed with many different friends; hiding from everyone. But my brothers came looking for me and found me one day. They gave me a good beating. They tied me up. They delivered me to my husband with my hands bound together and my legs held apart so he could consummate the marriage. I tried to escape again, then finally accepted my fate. I gave birth to a boy. He died a year later."

Source: International Center for Research on Women

* * *

Whether its causes are rooted in tradition, culture or poverty, forced child marriage leaves young girls vulnerable to abuse and deprivation. Their lives are given away for the benefit of others; all within the realm of societies which accept the practice as the status quo. Too young and powerless to object, they finally accept their destiny. They do not subject themselves out of weakness, but self preservation.

No matter what justifications their parents use, harming a child, taking away their liberty, their health and their education, is never normal or acceptable. And absolutely no rationale can justify the sexual abuse of a child, even within the context of a marriage.

Throughout the world, young girls are trapped in legal marriages in which they have absolutely no voice. With no one to help them or speak for them, they are shuttered away in lives full of misery and pain. Deserted by their families and friends, they quietly settle into a life of silent despair.

* * *

Twelve

I am Drissa

Hidden in Plain Sight

* * *

When Drissa was twelve years old, he decided to leave his village in Mali to look for work. With very few jobs available, there were many boys Drissa's age looking for paid labor in and the around the village. While it was difficult to leave his family and friends, he decided to cross the border into neighboring Cote d'Ivoire, where he heard there were many jobs available for people who did not mind hard work. When he arrived in Korhogo, he was pleased to be offered a good job on a cocoa plantation. Drissa agreed on the payment and work arrangements, and then went with the employment recruiter to begin his new job. Very suddenly, Drissa's new job turned into a nightmare. He and seventeen other boys on the cocoa plantation were forced to spend long days tending the cocoa plants and collecting the pods. Besides the back-breaking work, the heat was oppressive, the biting flies constantly swarmed around them, and they had to watch for snakes in the undergrowth. The bosses watching over them gave them little to eat, sometimes only braised bananas for months on end. Weak from hunger, they staggered under large sacks of cocoa pods. If they slowed in their work, they were beaten. At night the slaveholder locked them all into a small room with only a tin can to use as a toilet. Unwilling at first to believe what had happened to him, Drissa finally came to the awful realization that he had become a slave. Trapped, more than 300 miles from home in another country, far from any settlement, he did not even know exactly where he was. One evening before being locked in, Drissa attempted to escape. The slaveholder quickly caught him and savagely beat him. He still has the scars from those beatings. The next day, Drissa was forced to work, even though the wounds from the beating were still raw. Flies feasted on his exposed flesh. "We left our home for the promise of work and pay. The work is very hard and we are slaves of the cocoa industry. Now, only God knows our pain."

Source: Free the Slaves

* * *

According to the International Labor Organization (ILO), an estimated 246 million children are engaged in *exploitative child labor* worldwide. One of the most blatant forms of slavery, exploitive child labor or *forced child labor* is found everywhere in the world. The U.S. State Department's 2006 *Trafficking in Persons* Report lists 150 countries found to be "a source destination or transit country for trafficking of slaves." Almost three quarters of them work in hazardous environments such as mines or factories, or with dangerous substances such as chemicals and agricultural pesticides.

Operating outside of even the most basic labor laws, these children are forced into jobs that are often referred to as *3D Work: Dirty, Dangerous and Difficult.* Every day they are forced into painful work, long days in inhumane conditions without pay and with little food. "Their tiny spines already deformed like old men and women, their tender hands arthritic and calloused from their downtrodden labor, their lungs plagued by respiratory illnesses in poorly ventilated shops, the children are exploited in numerous physically, emotionally, and mentally exhaustive ways. Children who do not make their quota are beaten or thrown away," says Nina Smith, Executive Director of the Rugmark Foundation, an organization dedicated to ending child labor in the handmade carpet industry in South Asia.

They are made to carry chunks of coal up from deep Brazilian tunnels, to form dirt and clay bricks in Pakistan, to roll miles of woolen thread onto spools for hand-knotted carpets in Northern India, to harvest sugar cane in El Salvador, or to pick cocoa in West Africa's Cote d'Ivoire plantations. In India alone, UNICEF estimates the figure of children in hard labor at over ten million. In Pakistan, where children who labor in various forms of bondage number in the millions, sixty-seven percent are said to be involved in agriculture, eleven percent in carpet sectors, five percent in brick kilns, nine percent in wholesale and retail, eight percent in personal services. In Kathmandu, Nepal, thirty percent of a family's income comes from its children. According to the ILO, of the 2.6 million children aged five through fourteen in Nepal, forty-two percent are currently working regularly.

Like other forms of child trafficking, young children are often sold or deceived into their slavery. Working dawn to dusk, seven days a week, the children are forced to perform in their tasks until injury or ill health force them to stop. No longer of any use to the slaveholders, the expended child is simply thrown out; abandoned in the streets with no money, food or shelter. Young slaves remain with the slaveholder only if they are able to work at maximum levels, which may be a few months or several years.

Often, slavery continues through generations of families through a system called *debt bondage.* Enslavement begins with the impoverished parent's need for money. Out of desperation or mere indifference to the child, they indenture their son or daughter to a brick kiln owner, a rug loom manager or a cocoa plantation overseer for a set amount, sometimes as little as $15. They are not selling the child. They are borrowing money with the agreement that the child will pay off the debt. The child is both a commodity, exchanged between the parents and the employer, and collateral to secure the loan.

"Some evil in the world dies hard," says Gary Haugen, Director of the International Justice Mission. "Slavery is still with us because of debt bondage. The trick is, you can't get out of this debt unless you pay it off in a lump sum. But they're never paid enough to be able to meet that. And they are charged enormous interest rates, sometimes 500 percent a year, 1,200 percent a year. This is bonded child labor."

By creating a cycle of poverty and dependence, the slaveholders keep the uneducated and untrained slaves dependent in their debt bondage. Unable to obtain a wage-earning job when freed and discarded, the desperate victims often sell their own children into bonded labor for a tiny profit.

The parents are often destitute, using the loan to pay for food, meet family obligations such as a wedding, birth, funeral, or treat an illness. The employers use the loan to obtain the cheapest form of long-term labor possible. The child is forced into hard labor until the family's loan is paid in full.

Of course, this quickly becomes an impossible debt to settle as wages fail to meet the laborers falsified expenses such as bogus interest fees and living costs. The debt increases as the child becomes lost to a life of slavery.

* * *

Raman was born at the same brick kiln site where his father and grandfather had worked their entire lives to pay off a debt incurred by his grandfather. For 15 years, Raman and his family earned two cents per 80 kilogram bag of bricks to pay off the $450 advanced by the brick kiln manager years ago. They were beaten with sticks and hit by the owner if they were not working hard enough or producing enough bricks. They could not leave, because the brick kiln owner threatened to hunt them down and beat them or bribe the police into arresting them.

Source: U.S. State Department

* * *

Raman's story is not unusual for millions of children trapped in debt bondage. Working far from home, often in other countries, they are not allowed to attend school. Physical abuse is common while some are severely injured performing their duties. Many female bonded laborers are sexually assaulted by their owners. Often born into lower social status than other children, bonded labor predisposes millions of children to slavery, feeding a vicious cycle of generational exploitation. A child's inability to leave is also enforced by the widespread belief, held by parents and government officials, as well as employers, that the loan ought to be repaid .

In many industries, such as the hand rolling of beedi cigarettes in India, the child's labor does not pay off the original loan at all but only serves as interest on the loan and as a surety for its repayment. The original amount must still be paid in full. However, without schooling the children are typically illiterate; they have no way of knowing if the repayment is being accurately accounted for by their bosses. Varanasi, a twenty-year-old weaver in India, bonded since age seven, explained that if "they give us $2.08 a month, but write down $4.17, how will we know if we don't read and write? They'll write down a higher amount paid so that we owe them even more. They'll do it on purpose so that we'll remain bonded and be forced to keep on borrowing from them." These token salaries are further reduced for mistakes they claim the workers make, tools they use and often clothes they wear. The rate at which the debt is paid off is so slow and the salaries so small, families are often forced to borrow additional money just to survive, especially if the work is seasonal. Consequently, even if a loan is allegedly structured to be paid off by the child's labor, families never escape their debt or their slavery.

* * *

Ninety percent of West African cocoa plantations have slaves, meaning two-fifths of the world's cocoa is derived from slavery. Some victims wear dog collars and are referred to as "the creature" or "my slave." They work dawn until darkness, isolated from the world. They are unrecognizable when found. Locked in sheds at night, they urinate in buckets. If they try to run, they are beaten until broken. It is called the "breaking in period." After six months, they become resigned to their torture. If they are rescued, their psychological damage takes months or years to heal. If they break some minor discipline, their clothes are removed, they are thrown on the floor, hands tied, beaten with whips until their body is raw and covered by their tears. Some can never walk again. Flies infest the wounds. If they cannot walk, the slave masters then throw the person away. Ironically, the victims have never tasted chocolate.

Source: Free the Slaves

* * *

Over sixty-seven percent of cocoa beans come from West Africa, where the nation of Cote d'Ivoire provides forty-three percent of the world's supply alone. The United States is the largest importer of these same beans, where Americans spend $13 billion a year on chocolate. What many people do not realize is that this favorite delicacy is often produced by the forced labor of innocent young children.

According to detailed reporting from the ILO, approximately 286,000 children between the ages of nine and twelve work on cocoa farms on the Cote D'Ivoire alone, many as a result of child trafficking. Save the Children Canada reports that children are often trafficked from Mali, Burkina Faso, Togo and Benin, then brought into Cote d'Ivoire and other countries in West Africa. With world cocoa prices so low, many farmers maintain their cheap labor force through trafficking. Living in abject poverty, West African parents often sell their own children to cocoa farmers for $50–$100 in the desperate hope that the children will make some money on their own.

In 2001, motivated by negative publicity, the major chocolate companies agreed to a voluntary protocol to eliminate child labor on West African farms. Their alternative was to comply with new standards enforced through binding legislation from the U.S. Congress that would have required them to label their products "slave free," a qualification *none* of the major chocolate companies could meet.

The result was the *Harkin-Engel Protocol*, which established a four-year timetable for all levels and segments of the cocoa industry to adhere to standards set by the International Labor Organization. In July 2005, the Protocol quietly expired without any system in place to monitor or enforce adherence to its stipulations against slavery. The cocoa companies, who faced no repercussions for their inaction to *eliminate* child labor on cocoa farms, now claim they will *reduce* child labor by fifty percent in only two West African countries by 2008.

Bill Fletcher, president of TransAfrica Forum, a non-profit organization focusing on Africa states, "In order to ensure the profits that they wish, the companies are prepared to either accept or turn a blind eye to the use of child slaves or child laborers to do this work. If we are going to consume the chocolate, then it is incumbent upon us to understand and address the conditions of labor that bring it about."

As atrocities continue in the mass production of chocolate, "the cocoa farms are the tip of the iceberg," according to Jonathan Cohen, a researcher with the organization, Human Rights Watch. "Trafficking in child labor forces millions of young people to work day and night peddling goods in the market, fetching water, and caring for young children."

* * *

A man came and took me to a boat. On the boat, there were over 100 other children and some adults, but more children than adults. I talked to some of them, and all the girls were going to Gabon to work. It took three days on the boat to get to Gabon. The boat was very full. There were no toilets. There were girls defecating on each other and vomiting in the boat. It was impossible to vomit into the sea without falling off the boat. When we arrived the woman took us to her daughter and daughter's husband. Our job was to sell bread. There were two other girls living in the house doing domestic work. We sold bread in the market, circulating from six o'clock in the morning until night. At the end of each day we gave all the money to our boss. We were given about (ten cents) per day for lunch. At night we baked the bread for the next day. When we got home, our boss gave us the flour for the next day's bread. She showed us how to make the bread, and we did it with her and the two other girls. The boss was not nice to us. If we didn't sell all the bread in one day, she would beat us with a stick."

Ama, 12
Source: Human Rights Watch

* * *

Hidden in plain sight, *child domestic workers* are nearly invisible among child laborers. They work alone in individual households, far away from public scrutiny, their lives totally controlled by their employers. "Millions of women and girls turn to domestic work as one of the few economic opportunities available to them," says Nisha Varia, senior researcher for the Women's Rights Division of Human Rights Watch. "Abuses often take place in private homes and are totally hidden from the public eye."

Child domestics, nearly all girls, work long hours for little or no pay. Many do not attend school nor do they have any friends. They are subject to verbal and physical abuse, and are particularly vulnerable to sexual abuse. "Child domestic workers are unlikely to ever go to school, they have no control over their income, are subject to irregular working hours and face repeated insults, threats and violence," said Manab Ray, Manager of Save the Children's Child Domestic Worker project.

The ILO estimates that "domestic work in the households of families other than the child's own is the largest single employment category of under-sixteen-year-old girls in the world." Although it is difficult to know the exact number of girls forced into domestic service, it is likely to run into the millions worldwide. Yet, they have received little attention and even less protection. Government laws often exclude domestic workers from basic labor rights. Labor organizations rarely monitor or investigate conditions of work in private households, and few programs addressing child labor include child domestics.

According to Paulo Sérgio Pinheiro, appointed by the Secretary-General of the United Nations to study violence against children, child domestic workers report maltreatment such as "physical punishment, humiliation and sexual harassment. Most physical and psychological violence against child domestic workers is perpetrated by women, but girls are often subject to sexual violence from male members of the family of their employer."

Traffickers of children into the sex trade routinely deceive children and their families about what will happen to them by promising them attractive jobs as domestic workers. In the Philippines, the Visayan Forum Foundation has determined that most of the children and young women trafficked to Manila from rural areas in search of work are assured jobs as domestic workers, but in a significant number of cases end up in the sex trade. Sexual exploitation of child domestic workers due to the child's vulnerability and isolation in the homes of their employers is common. Studies conducted by Anti-Slavery International, a London-based human rights organization founded in 1839, show that:

- In Latin America, many boys who grow up in homes with female domestic workers often have their first sexual encounter with them.
- In Fiji, eight out of ten domestic workers reported that their employers sexually abuse them.
- In Haiti, *restavèk* girls are sometimes called "*la pou sa*," a Creole term meaning "there for that." These young girls are accepted sexual outlets for the men and boys of the households that hold them.

Finally, if a girl becomes pregnant, she is often thrown out of the house and forced to provide for herself on the streets. If this happens, and with few other options available, her domestic work is merely a prelude to prostitution.

* * *

Abak was just a baby when her parents were killed during a raid by a militia group in Sudan's decades-old civil war. When Abak fell from her slain parents' arms, she was somehow hidden in the rubble and commotion of the raid. The militia never found her. This was only the beginning. After being rescued by an aunt, Abak was abducted by the militia during yet another raid. She was snatched up and trafficked to the North of Sudan where she was held as a slave for ten years. There, she was forced to look after the slaveholder's children, clean the house and serve everyone in the family. She was never paid and was never allowed to go outside on her own. When Abak did not perform to her slaveholder's liking, he would threaten to sell Abak to someone in another country even further away from her village. She took these threats very seriously and always tried to please the slaveholder. Finally, a team of human rights workers was able to free Abak from her captivity, but even while free she has not entirely escaped the sense of fear and confusion. After a decade away from her community, she feels like a stranger in her own home. She has forgotten much of her native Dinka language, since the slaveholder forced her to speak Arabic, and her home village's customs and religious beliefs feel foreign to her. Abak says, "I am so happy to see my aunt again, and to be free, but now I do not know if I will ever feel at home again, no matter where I am." She says that her aunt encourages her to talk about the abuses she suffered as a slave, but that the words do not come. She has trouble sleeping at night.

Source: International Justice Mission

* * *

Children forced into domestic servitude are found everywhere and very little is done to help them. For instance, tens of thousands of young girls working as domestics in Morocco face severe physical and psychological abuse every day. According to Human Rights Watch researcher, Clarisa Bencomo, "Moroccan law denies these children basic labor rights, and the authorities rarely punish employers who abuse them." Her research demonstrated "girls as young as five working 100 or more hours per week, without rest breaks or days off, for as little as 70 cents a day."

Young and often illiterate, child domestic workers often lack the confidence and opportunities to leave abusive workplaces. They have no idea what exists outside the walls of the homes in which they work. Unfamiliar with the surrounding culture, language or terrain, they will languish in one home for years, reaching adulthood while living in slavery.

* * *

An orphan from an early age, Khalak worked on his uncle's small farm, taking the family cow every day to the jungle. One day, a family friend came in and offered to take him away from village life, saying that in Kathmandu, Khalak could go to school while working at his home. Once in the city, the man broke his promise and sold Khalak to a carpet master, who forced him to learn how to knot wool rugs on heavy wooden looms. Workdays started at 4 A.M. and went on until 11 at night. The earthen floor of the factory was Khalak's bed. When the owner had a rush order, Khalak and the other boys would have to work through the entire night. The owner was so strict that he even complained when Khalak had to relieve himself. Khalak never saw any money and never had a chance to play except when electricity failed.

Source: RUGMARK Foundation

* * *

If there is one aspect of forced child labor that has touched all our lives, it comes in the form of products made in sweatshops around the world. While many workplaces through history have been filthy, crowded and dangerous, providing only low wages and no job security, the concept of an industrial-age *sweatshop* began in the mid 1800s. This was a specific kind of factory in which an overseer, called a *sweater*, directed hundreds of people in producing cheap garments under terrible conditions.

Between 1850 and 1900, sweatshops attracted the rural poor to rapidly growing cities and attracted immigrants to growing urban centers in the United States and Great Britian. Often using children, these factories were cramped, poorly ventilated and prone to fires and rat infestations.

On March 26, 1911, The *New York Times* printed this front page story, "141 Men and Girls Die in Waist Factory Fire; Trapped High Up in Washington Place Building; Street Strewn with Bodies; Piles of Dead Inside Three stories of a ten-floor building at the corner of Greene Street and Washington Place were burned yesterday, and while the fire was going on 141 young men and women at least 125 of them mere girls were burned to death or killed by jumping to the pavement below."

Soon after the historic *Triangle Factory Fire* of 1911, child labor laws were enacted making it illegal to employ very young people in all but a very few occupations. While trade unions, minimum wage laws, fire safety codes, and labor laws have made sweatshops, today defined as any workplace that violates human rights, an infrequent occurrence in the United States and other developed countries, they continue operating in the developing world as an integral part of the global economy.

The demand for cheaper products has had a pejorative affect on the laborers, often the most expensive element in the production of consumer products. In order to supply the lowest prices to the largest number of people, manufacturers must output massive amounts of product at very little cost. Reducing labor costs is the best and most effective way of achieving higher productivity. In the last half of the 20th century, manufacturers discovered a goldmine of inexpensive labor in developing countries all over the world. These labor markets are comprised mostly of people who are desperate for wages of any kind, no matter how low. The resulting mass migration of manufacturing jobs out of the United States to countries providing labor at very low costs has not escaped public awareness. What has been hidden, for the most part, is that much of that labor is supplied by children; children who are forced to work as virtual slaves.

According to Linda Golodner, President of the National Consumers League, an advocacy group which has represented consumers on marketplace and workplace issues since 1899, the problem of child labor "has grown along with the expansion of the global marketplace. Child labor is cheap labor. Children are targeted for non-skilled, labor intensive work. Child workers are docile and easily controlled. Employers have no fear of children demanding rights or organizing."

Clothing sewn in China, for instance, is "usually done by girls who are forced to work seven days a week, often past midnight for only pennies an hour, with no benefits," according to Joseph T. Hansen, International President of the United Food and Commercial Workers Union. "The girls are housed in crowded, dirty dormitories, fifteen to a room, and fed little more than gruel."

The National Labor Committee *(NLO)*, a human rights organization which inspects working conditions in developing countries, has found that these workers are kept under constant surveillance and can be fired for merely discussing factory conditions. After quietly inspecting several factories, NLO reported that "many factories in China operate under a veil of secrecy, behind locked metal gates, with no factory names posted and no visitors allowed. China's authorities do not allow independent human rights, religious or women's groups to exist." Yet, this is where Americans acquire billions of dollars of goods every year.

The products made by very young workers are not at all limited to clothing. Handmade wool rugs are among South Asia's top export products and a high-employment sector for the poor. According to a 2006 report from UNICEF, fourteen percent of children in India age five through fourteen are engaged in child labor activities, including carpet production. "300,000 children are toiling in the rug trade in Pakistan, India and Nepal alone. Those three countries account for half of the $1.2 billion in sales of handmade rugs in the United States," reports Nina Smith of Rugmark. "They are subject to malnutrition, impaired vision and deformities from sitting long hours in cramped loom sheds. They suffer respiratory diseases from inhaling wool fibers and wounds from using sharp tools."

Some would argue that it is better for those living in poverty to work, no matter their age. They claim it will help the entire family with added income. In reality, according to UNICEF, The International Labor Organization and Rugmark, child labor actually makes poverty worse. Child workers cost manufacturers next to nothing or nothing at all, which directly decreases wages for adult laborers. The overall result is less income for families. Further, children who work forfeit an education that could help them achieve a higher standard of living as adults.

* * *

"I've been begging since I was eight," says Vamir. "My mother left when I was five, and I had no family to take me in. I started living on the streets of Beirut because I had no where else to go. Some men found me and told me they would give me food and a place to sleep if I went with them and begged for money on the streets in another city. They said

they would protect me. On the second day they said I didn't bring them enough money from begging tourists. So they beat me until I go and beg for more money."

Source: Integrated Regional Information Networks

* * *

In 1997, police in New York City found fifty-five deaf-mute children selling key-rings in the city's subway system. They had all been brought from Mexico by an organized crime gang specializing in trafficking. Upon investigation, the police learned that after working eighteen hours a day, each child was expected to bring their overseers $100. They were paid nothing and often subjected to violent physical abuse.

Whether it was on your way to a luxurious resort or making your way across any city in the world, you have probably encountered the street children. Often, these two settings are infused with or surrounded by poverty. This is where you encounter *children begging.*

This is certainly the closest most of us will ever come to children who have been exploited for the financial gain of others. Yet, after waving them off or driving away, it is easy to dismiss them and their situation. However, it only takes moment to ask some disturbing questions. Who organizes them into groups? Where do they get the small items they are selling? And why do so many seem to have some physical trauma or deformity?

The answers are very simple. They are collecting as much cash as they can for the people who forcefully send them out each day. These people train them, equip them, tell them where to go and, most terrifying of all, intentionally deform them to invoke more sympathy and money from those they encounter.

In Beirut, for example, many children "are forced to work as beggars by organized gangs, which pay them with cigarettes or drugs," said Jannot Sanah, a psychological supervisor at the Lebanese Evangelical Institute for Social Work and Development. In France, according to a report by The Protection Project, a human rights organization of Johns Hopkins University, "police have uncovered a series of criminal networks run by Romanian traffickers who recruit children and people with disabilities to beg on the streets of France or who even force people to pose as disabled." Further, they estimate "some 2,000 Romanian minors are begging on the streets of Paris and Marseille."

* * *

"More than fifty camels, with screaming children strapped onto their backs, would run." Ciaquat personally saw about twenty children die and more than a dozen injured every week. He recalls, "There was this one kid whose strap broke at the beginning of the race. His head was crushed between the legs of the running camel. Once the race has started it cannot stop."

Source: Child Workers in Asia

* * *

In 2004, investigative reporters from HBO used hidden cameras to document slavery and torture in secret desert camps where boys under the age of five were trained to race camels, a very popular national sport in the United Arab Emirates (UAE). They were able to expose a hidden child trafficking organization that bought or kidnapped hundreds of young boys in Sudan, Pakistan and Bangladesh and forced them to become camel jockeys in the UAE.

Rarely mentioned in western media, the issue of using trafficked boys as camel jockeys is well known throughout very wealthy Persian Gulf nations. Each year thousands of children, some very young, are used as camel jockeys. Deliberately starved to prevent weight gain, they live in camps, surrounded by barbed wire, near the camel racetracks. They are completely dependent on their captors for survival. Injuries are common. Many boys are crushed by falling camels and never receive medical treatment. In 2006, The U.S. State Department reported that in the UAE alone, "some boys as young as 6 months old were reportedly kidnapped or sold to traffickers and raised to become camel jockeys. Some were injured seriously during races and training sessions, and one child died after being trampled by the camel he was riding."

According to testimony given to Child Workers in Asia, by a child who was rescued after spending ten months in the UAE as a camel jockey, "They would take us and attach us with a cord to the camel's back, then they would make them run down a track covered in sand and boarded with large pointed iron posts and barbed wire. The camels had to run within the space, and the animals and children who fell were trampled by the frightened animals. Those who refused or who were scared were beaten and forced onto camels. We were very frightened of falling or dying."

Organized crime is not alone in fueling the industry of child trafficking for camel jockeys. In September 2006, a lawsuit was filed in U.S. district court charging that Dubai ruler and United Arab Emirates Vice President, H E Sheikh Mohammed bin Rashid Al Maktoum and his brother, Sheikh Hamdan bin Rashid Al Maktoum, had enslaved some 30,000 children since 1975 for use as camel jockeys. They are charged with "the alleged abduction and human trafficking of thousands of young boys" from places like Bangladesh, Sudan and southern Asia. According to the complaint "boys as young as two years old have been stolen from their families, trafficked across international borders, and kept in brutal camel-racing camps throughout the United Arab Emirates, forced to train camels and perform as jockeys."

* * *

"It's common for us business owners to exchange children. They are more obedient and work harder that way. We tie the child up for three or four hours to teach it not to run away. But those children who are very disobedient – of course such children have to be chained up and beaten."

Anonymous Carpet Factory Owner, Pakistan
From the film, *Stolen Childhoods*

* * *

"Child labor is the last form of slavery in the world," says U.S. Senator Tom Harkin. "A slave is someone who has no voice, no vote, no control over his own property. No control over his own livelihood. That's what these child laborers are."

Certainly, not all products made in developing countries are manufactured by children or under harsh conditions. But, how long would it take you to find just one product in your home that says, "Made in China" on the label? Consider all the products in your home, your office, your children's schools, and your local shopping mall, with labels from countries like Bangladesh, Ivory Coast, India, Pakistan, Taiwan. Are you certain of their *human* origin?

There are many awkward questions derived from our daily lives, if we dare ask them. It is nice to see the words "Hand Made" on the products we buy. It usually means higher quality. Yet, how small were the hands that made the shirt you are wearing right now? What did the child who made the rug in your living room eat today? Where did the child who processed the chocolate you ate yesterday sleep last night?

The answers are not at all convenient to live with. Whether or not we are willing to face our complicity, the answers, like the truths of forced child labor, are hidden in plain sight. The undeniable reality is that we are surrounded by the labors of children forced to make the objects of our desire.

* * *

Thirteen

I am Brisit

Why Shouldn't We Send Our Daughters?

* * *

"I met some girls on the street and I became friends with them. Two of the older girls used to work as prostitutes and give us the money to live. These people were good to me, so I followed them. I was really hurt by my family experience and these people were nice to me. I was afraid at first, but when I got used to it, I wasn't afraid any more. I'm familiar with people in the area. Everybody knows me, so there's no problem. I'm interested to stop my prostitution and find something else to do, but I don't know how to do anything else. Everybody has a different opinion about how to help, but we need a job, any kind of job."

Brisit, 13
Source: UNICEF

* * *

The demand for children's bodies is high. Simply stated, the exploitation of children is about money. It is a matter of economic survivability for some and a matter of pure greed for others. Like illegal drugs and weapons, children are commodities to all those involved in trafficking, from their parents, to the traffickers, to those who buy and use them.

There is nothing new about the trafficking of human beings. In 1904, the first Convention on Trafficking was held in Paris when European leaders became concerned about the trafficking of European and Asian women. During World War II, Nazi Germany trafficked gypsies, Jews, homosexuals, and many others to labor camps. At the same time, the Japanese trafficked Asian women for sexual slavery in military camps. While not motivated by profit or perversion, it can also be argued that the United States forcefully trafficked its own Japanese citizens to internment camps soon after the attack on Pearl Harbor.

The reasons for trafficking humans throughout history have not changed. The motive for financial profit runs strong in mankind. In every age and every culture, people have put aside their humanity in favor of their greed.

Since the industrial age began, many factors have led to children becoming victims of trafficking like never before. Children have been swept into the heap of human trafficking because of poverty, the attraction of a perceived higher standard of living in other areas, weak social and economic structures, a lack of employment opportunities, organized crime, discrimination, corruption, political instability, armed conflict, and cultural traditions.

Further, children are more vulnerable than adults. They do not know their rights. Afraid and alone, they can be easily tricked or coerced.

Primarily, the current onslaught of child victims is caused by poverty. For instance, most cities and towns with a thriving sex tourist industry suffer from widespread poverty. And poverty rarely exists in a vacuum. Illiteracy, cultural oppression, poor health, and political instability often accompany conditions of severe poverty. These areas become ripe for traffickers who use promises of higher wages and good working conditions in foreign countries to lure or buy children away from their families and into their networks. Young children leave their home, either by choice or force, to seek a better life elsewhere.

* * *

"I was raised by my grandmother in Mali, and when I was still a little girl a woman my family knew came and asked her if she could take me to Paris to care for her children. She told my grandmother that she would put me in school and that I would learn French. But when I came to Paris, I was not sent to school, I had to work every day. In their house I did all the work; I cleaned the house, cooked the meals, cared for the children, and washed and fed the baby. Every day I started work before 7 A.M. and finished about 11 P.M.; I never had a day off."

Reca, 14
Source: Free the Slaves

* * *

While poverty often provides the supply of children, profit is the motive that drives the market. A child can be resold and reused many times, producing cash with every transaction. Also, the low risk associated with the sale of children, taking place in areas of ineffective or non-existent law enforcement, make trafficking extremely profitable. Compared to the penalties for other criminal acts, the risks associated with it are negligible compared to the financial return. Another advantage is that unlike illegal drugs and weapons, child trafficking does not require a large capital investment, further reducing the risks. Finally, once in the possession of the trafficker, children can be used for any number of profit-making activities. "Trafficking usually involves long-term exploitation for economic gain. In some cases, the traffickers may profit even further by using the trafficked persons as manpower for other criminal purposes, such as selling drugs," reports Amy O'Neill Richards of the Central Intelligence Agency.

Poverty and profit are essential to understanding the overall causes of trafficking children. However, there are other important factors putting certain young people at risk.

Often, child trafficking flourishes simply because of an overabundance of available children; children who are suddenly orphaned or otherwise unsupervised. When warfare, disease and natural disasters devastate entire nations, it can destabilize and displace entire populations. In every instance, the most vulnerable, children, suffer the greatest. With no one to care for them, they are open to exploitation and abuse.

With thousands of children left orphaned by the Asian Tsunami of 2004, trafficking networks began to prey on children left alone by the tragedy. "Predators are always looking for ways to prey on the vulnerable, so it shouldn't surprise us that a disaster that creates victims and chaos has become a prime hunting ground for them," says Dr. Donna Hughes, author of *The Demand for Victims of Sex Trafficking*. "For exploiters," said Lisa Thompson, who directs anti-trafficking efforts for the Salvation Army, "any situation that leaves children homeless and orphaned is like the scent of a wounded animal to a wolf." Dr. Laura Lederer, who pioneered research on trafficking, echoes the same fears, "Places where there are political or economic instability, civil war or natural disaster are most likely to be targeted by traffickers."

In its annual study of international child workers around the world, the U.S. Labor Department reported that "natural disasters considerably increased the risk of child labor for vulnerable children in a number of Asian, African and Latin American communities." One of the worst examples of natural disaster fostering exploited children was in Pakistan, where an earthquake in October of 2005 killed more than 73,000 people. "Thousands of child survivors were orphaned or separated from their families, making them more vulnerable to trafficking and other forms of exploitative child labor," the Labor Department report said.

While increasing supply can flood the worldwide market with children, making them readily available for the sex trade or cheap labor, another reason for child trafficking is an increased demand. In August of 2006, the Salvation Army reported that it will work aggressively against human trafficking prior to the 2010 Soccer World Cup in South Africa. The organization said the event could see a dramatic increase in trafficking to supply prostitutes for the millions of fans who will attend. Several human rights organizations estimated that 40,000 prostitutes, many of them young girls, were trafficked into Germany for the 2006 competition.

In Chautara, a Tamang village north of the Kathmandu Valley, Chim Bamamang is a relatively wealthy man. His cottage is roofed with tin. His son's motorcycle is parked outside, next to the buffalo shed. Although he has no electricity, a television stands in the corner of the room, covered in cloth. "We will have electricity here in a few months," he says. Chim's prosperity is a result of his fortune to have fathered four daughters. Three are working in the brothels in Mumbai. The fourth, age twelve, will go next year. "Why shouldn't we send our daughters to help us?"

Source: Integrated Regional Information Networks

* * *

Discrimination against children based on gender, religious, racial or ethnic origins can also determine why some children are trafficked and others are not. In South Asian countries for example, the caste system is firmly rooted in the culture. Many teenage girls from India's Adivasi communities, viewed as a lower caste, are recruited in Jharkand and taken 350 miles away to work as domestic servants in Mumbai. "The girl is always restricted and kept inside, deprived of everything," says Camala, a young girl from Nepali.

Along with the caste system, the lower status of girls in some societies fuels the trafficking industry. Since the 1980s the increased demand for young women is a consequence of expanding gender gaps in India and China. Unwanted at birth, they are desired later as brides and concubines. In India, where 933 girls are born for every 1,000 boys, a female birth can be perceived as an economic liability. Often, couples use sonograms to determine the gender of the fetus, choosing abortion for females.

* * *

"They used to beat me and abuse me and say, 'We have spent money on you. You must entertain customers!' I continued to protest. This was even before I had reached puberty. We were never given condoms to use. Later, I got pregnant. I was forced to have sex right up to my ninth month of pregnancy. I had a daughter who survived only seven days. I had to entertain even when I had my period or if my genitals were swollen. I ran away once, but the police caught me and brought me back to the men. They said they would always find me and bring me back."

Source: Integrated Regional Information Networks

Trafficking would not exist to the extent it does today without the direct or indirect cooperation of law enforcement. The persistence of child slavery, especially in developing countries, is exacerbated by the weak rule of law. Easy and inexpensive corruption of government officials and police officers allow traffickers to operate with impunity. Because many build connections and clout over time they also know their victims will get little or no help from the local law enforcement if they escape. Though prevalent, corruption is not exclusive to poor countries. Japan has thousands of non-Japanese girls working in the sex industry. There, the police have been known to sell back the girls to traffickers if they escape, according to studies and interviews conducted by Human Rights Watch.

To further complicate the issue, even when the police are supportive of victims, the young people may not know if they can trust them, or anyone. Under the control of their captors for so long and constantly abused by so many adults, children often believe that seeking help will only bring them more suffering.

Because profits from child trafficking are so enormous, criminal organizations have been able to prosper. The growth of transnational crime syndicates' involvement in trafficking has led to an enormous expansion of black market economies. The growth of these economies as a substantial sector of a developing country's economy is often guarded by those even in the highest levels of government. Consequently, in many places around the world, traffickers "operate without fear of effective criminal sanction," says Gary Haugen, President of International Justice Mission. "This vast and brutal industry is able to operate only because it is tolerated by the civil authorities of the country."

Along with the belief that children are of little or no value, this is why so many nations have not taken the legislative or other governmental measures necessary to stop trafficking within their borders.

* * *

Fourteen

We are Bayla, Miliana, Flora, Karena . . .

Every Corner of the World

* * *

Bayla was nine years old when her father died. She was quickly left at an orphanage in Azerbaijan. But, knowing she could receive money for her Bayla's young life, her mother removed her from the orphanage and sold her to traffickers. The highly organized gang of criminals immediately moved Bayla to Dubai where she was prostituted in clubs until she was thirteen years old. After the Dubai police discovered her illegal status, Bayla was deported back to Azerbaijan. Once she returned there, however, she was prostituted for three more years before becoming pregnant. She contracted AIDS either in Dubai or in Baku and gave birth to an HIV-positive baby in 2005.

Source: U.S. Department of State

* * *

Child trafficking is global. Its shadow is cast upon every corner of the world. It happens in every country, every city, every culture and every religion. No one nation has a monopoly on evil or injustice; very few can point to their full history with complete pride. No one faith or ideology is immune or above the perils of human nature's darkest regions.

* * *

When Flora was thirteen, she was promised good work in a fabric factory just outside of Rome. Before leaving her native Nigeria, she underwent a voodoo ritual conducted by a friend of her mother. She was told the ritual was done to oversee her safety in Italy and ensure her loyalty to her sponsor. When she arrived in Rome, Flora was beaten by her sponsor, an older woman who told her she would have to repay a huge debt, incurred by her illegal transportation to Italy, through almost 4,000 acts of prostitution, "ten a day for a year." Flora received more beatings when she refused the woman's demands. Because she feared for her life and the lives of her family in Nigeria, she gave in. The very first day, she was beaten again for not earning enough money. When she became pregnant, Flora was forced to have an abortion.

Source: UNICEF

* * *

The exploitation of children is found everywhere on earth, from private homes to brothels and battlefields, from sweat shops to camel races and cocoa fields. Rich or poor, no nation is immune to the epidemic rise of child trafficking which, according to the U.S. Agency for International Development, "is a pernicious and brutal abuse of human rights that affects nearly every country in the world."*

* * *

* The condition of "nearly every country" instead of "every country" is almost always attributed to the fact that Antarctica alone has no reported cases of trafficking.

At the age of fourteen, Miliana was recruited by traffickers in Chiapas, Mexico who promised her a job working in a restaurant in Los Angeles. Even though the job did not pay much money, she thought she could help her mother financially while escaping from a violent household in which she was being secretly abused by her brothers. Professional traffickers arranged for her to be brought by smugglers from Mexico to Los Angeles. When she arrived, the traffickers took possession of Miliana and told her she would first have to work as a prostitute to earn enough money to pay back the smugglers who brought her there. Miliana was held captive in the house where she was forced to perform sex acts against her will and was continuously threatened that her mother in Mexico would be harmed if she refused to comply or tried to escape. After two months at her first location, Miliana and other young girls were taken to another location where she continued to be forced to work as a prostitute.

Source: Public Counsel

* * *

Across the world, tightly held rings of criminals, much like terrorist cells, are working diligently to supply the growing demand for children. They come with different names, different languages and different religions. But, they are all the same in the every evil way that matters.

* * *

After the Asian tsunami of 2004, Karena was looking for a job suitable for a young girl in Sri Lanka. "A very nice man became my friend and convinced me that I could find a much better job in Singapore as a waitress." The man arranged and paid for her travel. A Sri Lankan woman met Karena upon arrival in Singapore, confiscated her passport, and took her to a hotel. "The woman told me that I was now a prostitute and that I had to pay back the money it cost for me to be flown into Singapore. I was taken to an open space for sale in the sex market with other girls from Indonesia, Thailand, India, and China. We were inspected and purchased by men from Pakistan, India, China, Indonesia and Africa. The men would take us girls to nearby hotels and rape us." Karena was forced to have sex with an average of fifteen men a day. She developed a serious illness, and three months after her arrival was arrested by the Singaporean police during a raid on the brothel.

Source: Human Rights Watch

"No one signs up to be a sex slave," explains Theodore Romankow, President of the County Prosecutors of New Jersey, "but the problem of human trafficking exists everywhere. Sex slavery doesn't only occur in Third World countries or economically deprived countries. It's also a worldwide problem infesting countries such as Greece, Italy, Romania, China, Japan and even Canada and the United States."

Trafficking is a complex and multifaceted global crime against humanity. "The smuggling of migrants and the trafficking of human beings for prostitution and slave labor have become two of the fastest growing worldwide problems in recent years. Although the evidence suggests that trafficking in people is increasing everywhere, few traffickers are behind bars," states Antonio Maria Costa, Executive Director of the United Nations Office on Drugs and Crime.

Since the early 1990s, globalization has allowed multinational crime syndicates to expand their activities from drug and arms trafficking to human trafficking. Children, especially, have become the commodity of choice for global gangs taking every technological and geopolitical advantage to gain profits and power. Now, after only fifteen years of wild growth, we live in an age of transnational crime.

These worldwide organizations are able to adapt themselves rapidly to changing borders, political landscapes and legal restrictions. They operate with near impunity in a world where cooperation among the many nations in which they conduct their business is almost non-existent. While the diverse legal bodies combating them are balancing political struggles and various competing priorities, crime syndicates around the world are unified by the common priority of profit. They ignore borders, ethics, laws, and they buy, bribe or kill their way past anyone who stands in their way. Very simply, they are unified and operate freely anywhere in the world while the organizations fighting them are fractured and restricted to their own limited territory.

Even more advantageous to them, while the world focuses on the "War on Terror," the commercial exploitation of children is pushed far away from public scrutiny. These criminals and the children they destroy are simply not priorities to nations focused on other matters. Consequently, more than one million children a year are exposed to a *terror crime* against them.

As terrorism becomes the new warfare, it shares a common, awful trait with child trafficking. Both target the innocent. In these early days of the twenty-first century, the line between war and crime is becoming indistinguishable. Everywhere in the world, acts of war, terrorism and trafficking are raining down on our children, making almost every act of war a war crime.

Since exploitation, in all it forms, is perpetrated so lethally against children across the globe, perhaps it is time to view child trafficking as a form of terrorism. If so, would it be possible to combat the crime syndicates in the same way as terrorists? Are they not also responsible for the death of thousands of innocent victims each year?

They do not use guns, Improvised Explosive Devices or hijacked airplanes against adults. Their weapons, reserved for children alone, are far more personal. A knife to the throat. Rape. Starvation. Fear.

They do not share a common religious ideology. They do not pray or worship in a specific way. They are not motivated by nationalistic pride. They do, however, wield enormous power among the cities and nations of the world. Many of them are viewed as legitimate authorities and hold respectable places in their community. No matter their position, they are terrorists by any definition.

Certainly, as informed citizens, we can see the logic of preventing terrorist acts before they happen. Why then, do we not prevent them as they occur every day to thousands of the world's children?

* * *

"Some of us have wondered who is behind the children we see stretching their hands out to beg from grown-ups or running after them, calling out at people to buy something they are selling on the streets of Mumbai, Rio de Janeiro, Nairobi, Lagos, Lusaka, Maputo or somewhere else. Can any of the adults who brush by these children even imagine that, in every corner of the world, there are other children who cannot even be seen because they are

not allowed to talk to others or to be treated as children, or even to walk out of the places they are kept, regardless of their screams and tears? Alas, throughout human history's most tragic moments, during times of war, the slave trade and natural disasters, children have always been the ones to come off worst."

Graça Machel
Patron of the Southern Africa Campaign
Against Child Abuse and Child Trafficking,
Wife of Nelson Mandella

* * *

Each year, the U.S. Department of State's Office to Monitor and Combat Trafficking in Persons releases a study entitled the *Trafficking in Persons Report (TIP)*. The in-depth report is, according to State, "intended to raise global awareness, to highlight the growing efforts of the international community to combat human trafficking and to encourage foreign governments to take effective actions to counter all forms of trafficking in persons."

Accepted by the international community as the most reliable and comprehensive analysis of trafficking, TIP includes a comprehensive assessment of 150 nations and each government's level of compliance with the elimination of trafficking as outlined in the United States *Trafficking Victims Protection Act* of 2000 (TVPA), which is explained in Chapter 16. TIP details the efforts of these governments to protect victims and prevent trafficking within their borders by classifying each within a three-tiered rating system:

TIER 1 - Countries whose governments fully comply with TVPA's standards.

TIER 2 - Countries whose governments do not fully comply with TVPA's standards, but are making significant efforts to bring themselves into compliance with those standards.

TIER 3 - Countries whose governments do not fully comply with the standards and are not making efforts to do so.

There are several countries not ranked within this tiered system. Often, these nations are in great turmoil with no way to gain enough information to adequately report on child trafficking within them. Of course, without the rule of law human rights are immediately jeopardized. Trafficking in all its forms typically runs rampant. One such instance is Haiti, about which the TIP remarks, "An effective government must be put in place before Haiti can address its trafficking challenges."

* * *

"You just ask around town. People know who the scouts are. You just tell them what kind of child you are looking for and they can bring across whatever it is that you want."

Gilda P., Haitian Dominican Border Monitor
Jesuit Refugee Service.

* * *

Located closer to the mainland of the United States than Puerto Rico, the troubled nation of *Haiti* is a living nightmare for thousands of children. Haiti occupies the eastern half of the island of Hispaniola. The western half of the island, The Dominican Republic, is a haven for American tourists who visit the resorts that dot the coastline like enclaves of luxury amidst immeasurable poverty.

Travel a few hours by car from any of these beautiful vacation spots and you will come to a rugged border between the two countries. Along the way you will pass through countless poor Dominican villages, armed guards stopping you at the entrance to each. Approaching your car, one of the guards will ask to see your passport. Have it ready so you can hand it to him quickly and silently. Don't smile or making eye contact.

He will let his automatic rifle dangle off his shoulder as he looks at your papers. If you are lucky, your cab driver will explain to him that you are just passing through. But, since you don't speak the language, you really don't know what he's saying. Another guard stands in front of the car holding his gun. Between him and the front tires of your car is a long, heavy stick, perhaps eight feet in length. Someone has nailed hundreds of spikes into the stick. Any vehicle passing over it will immediately blow all its tires.

After a few moments, the man at your window signals his friend with a small wave of his hand. While the big stick gets lifted out of the roadway, clearing your path to drive through, your passport is handed back. You drive away hoping the checkpoint at the next village is just as easy.

Upon your arrival at the border with Haiti, be prepared to wait and spend some money. The border guards on the Dominican Republic side are moody and don't want any hassles or trouble. You do what they say and give them what they want. Corruption on the border between Haiti and the Dominican Republic is a major factor in the prevalence of trafficking between the two countries. Through their research conducted over a one year period, the International Organization for Migration and UNICEF found that Dominican border officials readily accept bribes in exchange for allowing traffickers to bring Haitian children into the Dominican Republic.

The border guards on the Haiti side are easier to deal with. There aren't any.

Once you cross into the Haitian villages along the border, you are on your own. If you get into trouble don't look for a phone, or electricity, or a hospital. Only filth and desperation. And the police won't help you. In fact, it's better to avoid them altogether.

This is a nation of severe poverty and corruption. To say that it is a land of horrible injustices does not begin to clearly explain the situation of its people. Living within all of this are children with no one to protect them.

Child exploitation flourishes in Haiti. Ninety minutes away from Disney World, tens of thousands of children live as restavek, or child slaves. In Haiti, a restavek is an undocumented, unpaid, unprotected, live-in child domestic worker. A child is often given or in some way sold to another family in order to become their lifelong servant. This removes the financial burden of caring for the child by their biological family while perhaps providing some income if a transaction takes place for possession of the child.

Poverty is the fundamental cause of the restavek system, which may have begun after Haitian independence in the early nineteenth century. Since then, one corrupt government after another has not changed the destitute conditions there. Eighty percent of Haiti's population lives in poverty, according to the United Nations. The average family income rarely exceeds $250 a year, an amount which must feed, clothe, and shelter an average of four or five children. Most of the population is young, forty percent are under fifteen years old, and most Haitians die before fifty. Almost half of Haiti's families are headed by single women who have no sustainable income.

"Child slavery in Haiti may be the ultimate symbol of a state that has failed its most vulnerable members," states Jocelyn McCalla, Executive Director of The National Coalition for Haitian Rights.

The U.S. State Department considers Haiti, "a source, transit, and destination country for men, women, and children trafficked for the purposes of sexual exploitation and forced labor. The majority of trafficking in Haiti involves poor mothers giving custody of their children to more affluent families." Further, State recognizes that the restavek system "is widespread and often involves sexual exploitation, physical abuse, and youths being subjected to conditions of involuntary servitude.

UNICEF estimate between 250,000 to 300,000 children are restaveks and that up to 3,000 Haitian children are trafficked to the Dominican Republic each year.

The language spoken by most Haitians is Creole. Perhaps the restavek can be explained best by an old proverb from that language which says, "Children are the unfortunate goods of the poor."

* * *

"Have you tried the nightlife here? If you want anything, you should come to me. I can get you girls. Any sort you want. Nice young girls, but experienced. They'll do anything you want. Just let me know and I'll arrange it for you."

Costa Rica Restaurant Waiter
Source: BBC

* * *

Haiti is certainly not alone in its use of children in this region of the world. Well organized child sex industries exist freely throughout all of Central and South America. There is very little any one of these nations can do to prevent it. As authorities implement effective programs to fight child trafficking in one country, the exploitive business quickly shifts to another with fewer legal measures against it. With a flood of eager customers from the north, this region has seen a dramatic and steady increase of sex tourists since the mid-1990s.

Along with sexual exploitation, children in Central and South America are also used for forced agricultural labor, domestic servants and soldiers.

In 2006, the U.S. State Department lists twenty Central and South American nations that do not comply with the minimum standards necessary to protect children from trafficking. Among them are such popular American tourists' favorites as Brazil, Mexico, Costa Rica, Dominican Republic, and Jamaica.

* * *

"In China, they sell you again and again. Young girls are sold to bars. Women are sold to farmers, and then resold."

Tung Ae
Source: *The Washington Post*

* * *

Discuss the topic of slavery today and most people consider it a matter of history. Considering it a thing of the past, they dismiss the subject as something that ended in Lincoln's era. Ironically, slavery does belong in a historic context since "the largest slave trade in *history*" exists *today* in Asia, according to Kul Gautum, Deputy Executive Director of UNICEF.

Today, however, trafficking is conducted using "even more cruel and devious means than the original slave trade," Gautum says. Further, UNICEF and Free the Slaves have determined that more than 30 million children have been traded over the last three decades throughout Asian countries.

In Myanmar, commonly known as Burma, victims are often trafficked along jungle paths to Thai villages. Children are trafficked to Australia, China, Singapore, and Taiwan. Myanmar also serves as a transit point for Chinese girls trafficked to northern Thailand and as a destination for girls from Vietnam. Additionally, children are trafficked internally within the country to serve as soldiers.

In Laos, children are being trafficked from Laos to Hong Kong, Japan, Malaysia, and Thailand, as well as to North America. Chinese victims are taken through Laos en route to Europe and the United States, and Vietnamese girls are trafficked through Laos en route to Thailand.

* * *

"Our life was difficult there. It was hard to earn money," Briana says. At the age of thirteen, her parents felt it was time for her to start making a living to support her younger sisters and brother. Briana's parents contacted a recruiter who found work for young people in Manila. "I didn't want to go to Manila, but my parents wanted me to. I told them I was too young, but they said it would not be noticed and that I could pass for eighteen. The recruiter had already paid my parents about $10. I told them to return the money to the recruiter, but they had already spent it." Briana started working for the family of a police officer. He raped her twice. "I begged him to send me back to the recruiter. He agreed on condition that I keep quiet about the attack on me. If I didn't, he said he would kill me." Briana eventually told her recruiter what happened. "But his response was simply, 'So, you were raped. Become a prostitute.'"

Source: Free the Slaves

* * *

In the Philippines, "300,000 Japanese take sex tours there every year," according to Dr. Mohamed Mattar, Executive Director of The Protection Project.

In Thailand, while the exact number is difficult to track, UNICEF estimates the number of Thai children involved in prostitution is between 60,000 and 200,000. "The young girls have encountered corrupt police and have seen how they abuse their victims," explains Sister Supaporn Chotipal, Director of the Fountain of Life Center in Bangkok. "Some trafficked girls are involved in the drug trade which makes their situation very dangerous. They have seen the violence inflicted on other girls who have tried to escape from the gangs. They are also aware of the powerful network that their abusers have and know that they will be found in just a short time if they try to escape."

"The magnitude of the problem in Asia almost defies belief, with hundreds of thousands trafficked annually, primarily for sexual exploitation and forced labor," states a report from the U.S. Agency for International Development Office of Women in Development.

* * *

People laugh about prostitution being the oldest job in the world, but I've seen so many awful things. Girls are chained up and beaten with electric cables; one had a nail driven into her skull for trying to escape. Another, Thomdi, was sold to a brothel when she was nine. When I saw her in the street she was seventeen and sick with AIDS and TB. She had lots of abscesses and the people at the hospital insulted her and refused to take her in.

Somaly Mam, Director
Acting for Women in Distressing Situations

* * *

In Cambodia, brutality is the result of decades of war, corruption, totalitarianism and genocide. Still scarred from the deadly dictatorship of Pol Pot in the 1970s, Cambodia remains one of Asia's poorest nations. As a result, the life of a child is not worth much. Children in Cambodia are mostly trafficked internally for use in the huge sex tourist trade which attracts pedophiles from all over the world. Also, according to Interpol, victims for the sex tourists are trafficked in from other countries such as Vietnam, Thailand, and as far away as Romania and Moldova.

Somaly Mam, Founder and Director of the Cambodia-based human rights organization, Agir pour les Femmes en Situation Précaire, translated as Acting for Women in Distressing Situations, was orphaned when she was nine years old. Unwilling and too poor to care for the child, her grandparents sold her into slavery. She can remember working for several families as a domestic servant. Treated poorly by each, she would work day and night catering to the whims of her masters. Then, one of the families sold her to a brothel. From that point on she was forced to service several foreign clients every day. She recalls, "Once a client took me and another girl; he said he was with just one other man. In fact, there were twenty of them; they treated us so badly I wanted revenge. I wanted to kill the man who took us."

This went on for eight years, until she was able to escape.

After struggling to cope with what had happened to her as a child, Somaly Mam returned to the streets where other girls continued to be abused. There she helps young girls to escape and fights the brothel owners and corrupt government officials who allow the child trafficking and exploitation to flourish. When people ask if her work is rewarding, she tells them, "When I close my eyes I feel raped and dirty. I'm very weak. At night when I don't sleep, I think that right at that moment many children are being raped. The pills I used to take don't work any more. But I can get by with two or three hours' sleep. I don't know what being happy means. But I like seeing the girls smile. That makes me feel good."

With no official help, Somaly frequently conducts raids on the streets of Phnom Penh, Cambodia's capital, where brothels are plentiful and full of pre-pubescent and adolescent girls living in filthy conditions. After a successful raid, Somaly can flee to her secretly located safe-house with dozens of girls. Obviously, the work is extremely dangerous, but for Somaly, "meeting a politician is much worse than having a gun pointed at me. I didn't go to school, I don't find it easy to talk and behave properly with a bureaucrat. I have to say the truth, which hurts, but if you don't tell the truth, nothing changes."

* * *

In the middle of a street in Jangback, three men dressed as Chinese authorities, grabbed me and threatened me. They dragged me to a house in a remote rural village. Two other North Korean girls were already detained there. None of us spoke Chinese. The Chinese men kept a very close watchful eye on us. They beat and raped us on a daily basis, myself included. During the one month I was detained, acts more humiliating and shameful than I had ever imagined possible, were forced upon me. I realized that the people who had captured me are not Chinese authorities but human traffickers, kidnapping and selling North Korean girls to Chinese people.

Source: Freedom House

In North Korea, famine, oppression, and the forced indoctrination into the cult of "Dear Leader" Kim Jong-Il have been a way of life for generations. Very little information, or anything else, escapes this extremely isolated and desolate country.

The United Nations estimates more than two million people died during the 1995–1998 famine in North Korea. Along with systematic corruption and abuse, the famine caused an exodus of North Koreans into China in search of food and work. Since that time the migration north has never ended.

While some of those fleeing into China are refugees escaping persecution from the Kim Jong-il government, the majority of North Koreans crossing the border are young women trying to survive and earn money to send back home. The situation has become so desperate that they are willing to risk their lives to help their families.

Kim Choong-ae and her twelve-year-old daughter, Kim Tee-kyun, are from Pyongyang, the capital of North Korea. After their second escape from North Korea, they were assisted by workers from Anti-Slavery International, who interviewed them about their first escape attempt. "To get into China, we crossed the icy Tumen River in the middle of the night. During the first month, my daughter was abducted from the house where I worked as a nanny. She was sold for $480 and forced to marry a man in a remote rural village. To get her back, I had to pay the man. I bought my daughter back. After two years in China, four men came to our house at night and kidnapped us. They were planning to sell us as brides to men in a mining town. The neighbors, suspecting foul play, called the police. My daughter and I spent forty days in a Chinese detention center before being deported to North Korea. In North Korea, we were stripped naked, checked for hidden money and sent to a labor camp on the border. My daughter was beaten and interrogated. All we had for food was porridge made from black, rotten flour and watery soup. We worked in the cabbage patches and carried heavy wood from the mountains. The guards threw stones at us if we weren't quick enough."

In 2006, The U.S. Department of State lists North Korea, along with the Asian nations of Burma and Laos, as a Tier 3 nation because "thousands of North Korean men, women, and children are forced to work and often perish under conditions of slavery inside the country. Thousands of North Koreans, pushed by deteriorating conditions in the country, become economic migrants who are subjected to conditions of debt bondage, commercial sexual exploitation, and/or forced labor upon arrival in a destination country, most often the People's Republic of China."

* * *

"At 4:00 A.M. I got up and did silk winding. I slept in the factory with two or three other children. We prepared the food there and slept in the space between the machines. The owner provided the rice and cut the cost from our wages. We cooked the rice ourselves. We worked twelve hours a day with one hour for rest. If I made a mistake, if I cut the thread, he would beat me. Then he would give me more work."

Retammae, 11
Bonded in India for $35
Source: Human Rights Watch

* * *

In India, with a total population of over *one billion* people, millions of children work and live as virtual slaves, unable to escape the treachery that will leave them impoverished, illiterate, and often crippled by the time they reach adulthood. These are bonded child laborers, often called "Dalits" or *untouchables*. Bound to their employers in exchange for a loan, they are unable to leave until the debt is paid, yet they earn so little they will probably never be free. The Indian government knows about these children and has established laws to free them. However, with apathy, caste bias, and corruption, most officials deny that they exist at all.

Somewhere between 60 to 115 million children are working in India, according to the International Labor Organization; some in agriculture jobs, others are picking rags, making bricks, polishing gemstones, rolling beedi cigarettes, packaging firecrackers, working as domestics, and weaving silk saris and carpets. Since 1995, efforts in some areas have driven bonded child labor out of factories and into households because they are partially exempt from the law. This has merely changed how bonded child labor works, but not its prevalence or cruelty. In many areas, bonded child labor is still practiced openly.

Indian silk production is especially difficult and dependent on children. "Boiling cocoons, hauling baskets of mulberry leaves, and embroidering saris, children are working at every stage of the silk industry," states an in-depth study by Human Rights Watch. "Conservatively, more than 350,000 children are producing silk thread and helping to weave saris." In order to meet the demand for silk in India (the world's largest consumer of silk), the United States (second largest) and the rest of the world, children work twelve or more hours a day, six and a half or seven days a week, under conditions of physical and verbal abuse. Starting as young as age five, they earn from nothing at all to around $8.00 a month, some or all of which is deducted against loans ranging from $20 to $200.

* * *

"This is the thing that God blessed me with, so I have to work like this. I can't do something else. . . . It is written on my head and nobody can change this. I am born into this community so we don't know what else to do. We have to do this and nothing else. I don't want to go to the looms, but there is no other way."

Vimatli, 15
A low-caste girl, bonded to a loom owner for $167

* * *

Wherever silk thread is made in India, children are being injured from machines and sharp threading systems. They are made to boil cocoons, inhaling smoke and diesel fumes from the ovens. The poor ventilation causes respiratory ailments such as chronic bronchitis and asthma. They must put their hands in scalding water to cook the dead worms, making their hands raw, blistered, and infected.

While observing the conditions in which these children work, Human Rights Watch investigators interviewed twelve-year-old Bashneer about his work in a silk reeling facility, "Boiling water falls on your hand.

You are always in water, standing in it. The skin on your hands and feet peels off. It gets loose." Anesa, eleven, started working when she was nine. Looking at the lumpy scars on her hands she explains, "I didn't like working because I got holes in my hands and they would get infected. I couldn't use my hands to eat." Her shins, ankles, and feet are also covered with burn scars from boiling water. Bashneer and Anesa are among the fortunate few. They were rescued from the slavery of their bonded labor and are now studying, safely, in a small private school.

* * *

"Children are very compliant. They don't demand minimum wage or create unions. You can lock them up and keep them from going home. Adult laborers take breaks for lunch, to smoke, but children will work the whole day without breaks. They are seen by their keepers as more efficient workers. They are afraid of the employer and of their parents, so they just do as they are told."

Varanasi
Educational Director for Indian Schools educating former child laborers

* * *

Like many other countries in Asia, forced child labor is not the only form of child trafficking and exploitation in India.

Child sex tourism is increasing dramatically. "Foreign tourists are frequenting India because of its relaxed laws, abundant child prostitutes and the false idea that there is a lower incidence of AIDS," states Rahul Bedi, the New Delhi correspondent for *Jane's Defense Weekly*. Because of the enormous land mass and population, ending the widespread practice of child sex tourism is difficult to manage. As one popular area for pedophiles is discovered by authorities, allowing for protection and prevention efforts to take place, child sex tourists and the criminals who traffic the children simply choose another area for their destination. They are able to make changes quickly and use the internet to communicate the latest information.

The reasons for child sex tourism flourishing in India are complex. Certainly, poverty is a major factor, but there are deeply rooted cultural causes as well. In general, child sex tourism is not seen as a major issue in India. According to Joseph Gathia, author of the book, *Child Prostitution in*

India, the social acceptability of sex with young people is "largely ignored because large scale child marriage still takes place. In addition, women from a number of social groups are considered 'inferior' and their sexual exploitation is not considered as 'something wrong' in a portion of Indian society. The women and girls of Dalit and Adivasi communities are termed as 'loose' and therefore free for all to sexually exploit."

* * *

"I am really scared of the police. They ask for money, which I don't have. I don't know what to do, I am all alone."

Bhanjana, 12
Source: New Delhi Television News

* * *

"In India, the abuse of both male and female children by tourists has acquired serious dimensions," sites a research study conducted by the United Nations, the National Human Rights Commission and the Institute of Social Sciences. The study surveyed 4,000 people across twelve Indian states, including traffickers, victims and survivors of commercial sexual exploitation, clients, brothel owners, and police officials. The report found that "unlike Sri Lanka and Thailand, this problem has not been seriously tackled or discussed openly in India and has remained more or less shrouded in secrecy, making the likelihood of child abusers being caught and punished very low."

India also serves as an example for one of the most grotesque uses of children, organ harvesting. Though India banned commercial trading in human organs in 1994, Nancy Scheper-Hughes, Director of Organs Watch warns that regulations quickly pushed India to the center of "an even larger underground market controlled and organized by cash-rich crime gangs expanding out from the heroin trade into the organs trade, making India a veritable organs bazaar operated out of private clinics."

This kind of illegal activity does not take place in a vacuum. It requires a well orchestrated group of individuals motivated by profit. According to the late Dr. A.K. Tharien, founder of the Christian

Fellowship Hospital in Tamil Nadu, "the commercialization of organs in India has been taking place through an organized network involving hospitals, doctors, criminals and agents."

* * *

"It seems like we Russian women are placed in impossible economic conditions and are not needed by our own country. In other countries, we are spit on as prostitutes when we are really victims. Ten years have passed since I was trafficked but the situation has still not changed. Is the German government really not aware of what is happening in their country? Or are they happy to profit from our suffering?"

Tasha, held captive in a German prostitution ring,
Testimony before the Global Human Rights and
International Operations Subcommittee
of the U.S. Congress

* * *

Europe is second only to Asia according to the U.S. Department of State's estimates of persons trafficked annually. After the opening of the region's borders subsequent to the collapse of the USSR, cultural and governmental transition brought high unemployment and poverty, rampant corruption, dislocation and, in many instances, violent conflict.

Europe is also home to some of the most vicious transnational crime syndicates. Using the disorganization and corruption of former Soviet States, they have created a global industry of child trafficking, especially young girls for sexual exploitation. They move trafficking victims to Western Europe from source countries in the east, with Albania, Moldova, Romania, Russia and Ukraine among them. "We're seeing is a lot of young persons trafficked within the region and sold into begging, prostitution and forced labor," says Lars Loof, Director of the Children's Unit of the Council of Baltic Sea States. "In Austria, for example, gangs have been caught importing children as young as ten from Romania and Moldova and forcing them to beg and steal."

The expansion of the European Union has also facilitated child trafficking by bringing its borders closer to economically unstable countries such as Ukraine, Albania, and Moldova.

As the USSR began to collapse in the last decade of the 20th century, the Republic of *Moldova* declared independence and formed a democratic government dedicated to free-market reforms. From the outset, however, an ineffective parliament, violent separatist movements, a lack of natural resources, and widespread criminal activity, combined to make this Eastern European nation's transition to democracy extremely difficult.

Approximately the size of the state of Maryland, it is the poorest nation in Europe.

In 2006, at least 500,000 of Moldova's 3.6 million people have left the country in search of work, according to Vladimir Lozinski, in a report prepared by UNICEF. In the wake of these migrations, are an estimated 40,000 children who are separated from both parents. "Some of these children live with relatives or neighbors, while others are left in the care of institutions. In the tiny village of Rublenita, sixty percent of the working population has left for Russia or Italy," says Lozinski.

"Moldova has become one of the main countries of origin for trafficking victims," says UNICEF Assistant Project Officer Angelina Zaporojan-Pirgari. Though the precise number of children trafficked from Moldova and other countries in the area is unknown and data are unavailable from local authorities, the Temporary Centre for Minors in Moscow estimates that more than 50 per cent of the children begging on Moscow streets are from Moldova.

According to the U.S. State Department, "Moldova is a major source country for trafficking in women and girls for the purpose of sexual exploitation. Victims are trafficked throughout Europe and the Middle East, increasingly to Turkey, Israel, the U.A.E., and Russia." In some cases, Moldovan girls are found even further away from home. In March 2003, the Japanese Interior Ministry's Department on Human Trafficking discovered a network based in Chisinau, Moldova, that trafficked young women from Moldova to work in nightclubs in Japan. The network was led by a thirty-year-old woman who recruited girls through ads published in local newspapers.

Moldova serves as a prime example of other nations experiencing higher levels of child trafficking. Researchers at the Institute for Public Policy, found that "the single most important factor that contributes to the problem of child trafficking is widespread poverty." Their research shows that in 2004, more than fifty percent of the population lived on less than $30 per month.

* * *

"I asked my friend Claudine to help me. We went to a bar and she told a man that he could take me home for the night. Now, when I don't have a client, I don't get any food and I cannot pay the rent. A lot of policemen and military personnel are clients themselves. Sometimes the girls get beaten up by the policemen. There is no place for them to turn when they get attacked like that."

Félicienne, 14
Source: UNICEF

* * *

Both of Félicienne's parents were killed during the 1994 genocide in Rwanda. She lives in Gisenyi, a town in the north-west section of Rwanda, with her younger sister, Umotoni and brother, Justin. Since she was eight years old she has fought to provide for the three of them. According to Save the Children, there are 65,000 children in Rwanda who have been orphaned and have to care for younger family members. Many become involved in prostitution to try to provide for themselves and their younger siblings.

Today there are large areas of the world with absolutely no government or laws in place. Most of them are in *Africa*. Without a functioning government, or any working, reliable legal authority to carry out law enforcement, corruption and anarchy rule.

Desperate crises associated with civil and interstate wars in Sudan, Somalia, Liberia, Sierra Leone, Rwanda, Burundi, Angola and the Democratic Republic of Congo have produced deaths on a genocidal scale, massive migrations across borders, and the untold suffering of millions of children.

Warfare is not the only problem brought to bear upon Africa's children. Although HIV/AIDS has affected populations throughout the world, the situation in Africa is by far the most dangerous. The twenty-one countries with the highest prevalence of HIV are all in Africa. The United Nations has determined that the sub-Saharan Africa region has the fastest growing HIV/AIDS epidemic with seventy percent of all global infections. They also found that at least ninety-five percent of all AIDS orphans, children who have lost both parents to the disease, are African. A UNAIDS study on the global HIV/AIDS epidemic reported that the number of children who became orphans because of HIV/AIDS worldwide was fourteen million out of which eleven million are in the sub-Saharan African countries. "Some children are double victims of AIDS: first when their parents die from the disease, and then when they are trafficked and subjected to likely HIV infection," says Jonathan Cohen, an HIV/AIDS researcher for *Human Rights Watch*.

With nothing to protect them against the duel threat of open warfare and AIDS, children are losing their battle to survive in Africa.

* * *

"There are young people who have been profoundly hurt by the violence of adults: sexual abuse, forced prostitution, involvement in the sale and use of drugs; children forced to work or enlisted for combat; young children scarred forever by the breakup of the family; little ones caught up in the obscene trafficking of organs and persons."

Pope John Paul II

* * *

Having already discussed the situation of children being trafficked and forced into military service or slavery to process cocoa, it is important to recognize the other situations throughout the continent.

In Sudan, the north-south war, which killed two million people and forced more than four million to flee their homes, left hundreds of thousands of children who were without supervision or protection. In 2006, the American public was finally made aware of a separate conflict which has decimated the western region of Darfur, where violence continues.

In Zimbabwe, operation *Restore Order* is referred to by the people as *Zimbabwe's Tsunami*. Beginning in 2005, the project, which placed "a significant number of its citizens at risk for trafficking," according the U.S. State Department, demolished thousands of homes and businesses. According to state, "An estimated 223,000 children were affected and left vulnerable to trafficking." A United Nations report says that the operation is a "disastrous venture carried out in an indiscriminate and unjustified manner, with indifference to human suffering."

In Liberia, fourteen years of civil war have left the country in ruins. Angela Kearney, UNICEF's Liberia Representative, says the civil war in that country caused "a breakdown in the very fabric of society which left children with nothing. Many schools are destroyed, many teachers have left. Vaccination campaigns haven't happened. We are very concerned about the threat of HIV/AIDS."

In Somalia, the people have been without a central government since 1991 and the situation there is desperate. "The whole of the eastern African region is suffering from drought and a shortage of food," reports Dom Nutt of Christian, an association of churches in the United Kingdom and Ireland. "Somalia is a particular case because while there is no pasture, there is no water, there is no food for most people, there is also the added problem that Somalia has no government to talk of and there is no rule of law." Kenya's Minister for Foreign Affairs Raphael Tuju, told the UN General Assembly, "A Somalia with no government in place is a danger not just to neighboring countries but to the whole world."

In Lesotho, thirty-one percent of the adult population has AIDS. If the same proportion were true for the United States, 93,000,000 people would be infected. Very few people know of Lesotho, which has a population of 2.2 million. About the size of the state of Maryland, this nation is completely surrounded by the Republic of South Africa. AIDS poses "a threat to every sector of society from the economy to education to the health system," according to the Lesotho Transformation Resource Centre. AIDS, they report, "produces a huge number of orphans and child-headed families." Further, a 2005 UNICEF report refers to women running child brothels in exchange for provision of food and shelter.

In Swaziland, the AIDS situation is just as bad as Lesotho. By 2010, UNICEF predicts that Swaziland will have 110,000 orphans under the age of fifteen. The forecast also state that the population at that point will decrease from 950,000 in 2006 to 700,000 due to AIDS. In 2010, the orphan demographic will be one of the largest sections of society. "Human vultures will descend to prey on these children," states Pastor Jabulani Dlamini, a social researcher in Swaziland. "Unless there is an accounting for every child, they may be swooped up by child traffickers, never to be seen again."

* * *

Gina, 15, was convinced by a man she met to run away from her family in Chicago and come to Ohio. "The dream he sold me was that he had this place in Cleveland, and I could do better there. I could live in a big house and get away from my family. I just had to work hard." Arriving at the man's house, Gina found many other girls her age living there. Immediately she was given over to the pimps who forced her into a brutal initiation process. Like every new girl who came to the house, she was beaten, locked in a closet and raped. Then, when they were thoroughly submissive from abuse, every girl became a sex slave servicing several customers a day. "They take you to a certain city and they put you on a block where you have to be out and soliciting people, but that's about as much as you know." The cache of very young girls was being moved from state to state, through truck stops and into motels, anywhere they could be sold to customers and earn money for the pimps who held them as slaves in America.

Source: Polaris Project

* * *

Most Americans consider child trafficking as something that occurs in other parts of the world. "This is a crime of hidden victims," says John Rabun, Vice President of the National Center for Missing & Exploited Children. "Many think child trafficking is only a problem in foreign countries, but nothing can be further from the truth."

The Federal Bureau of Investigation reports that thousands of children are brought into the United States every year explicitly for sex work and that child trafficking occurs in virtually every state. "In an era of improved technology, it has become much easier for traffickers, and their victims, to move freely across borders," says Attorney General Alberto R. Gonzales. "Trafficking is now a transnational criminal enterprise that recognizes neither boundaries nor borders."

"Neither slavery nor involuntary servitude, except as punishment for crime whereof the party shall have been duly convicted, shall exist within the United States, or any place subject to their jurisdiction."

Thirteenth Amendment to the Constitution
December 6, 1865

* * *

Only *legal* slavery was ended by the Thirteenth Amendment to the U.S. Constitution. Like all other illegal activities for which there is still a demand, the business simply moved underground. Because of the clandestine manner in which the traffickers now move people into and across *America*, it is nearly impossible to determine the exact number of victims. However, in 2005 the U.S. Department of State and the Central Intelligence Agency estimated that, "50,000 people are trafficked into or transited through the United States annually as sex slaves, domestic servants, garment slaves and agricultural laborers."

Human trafficking victims may be anywhere, "including living down the block or sitting next to you in church this weekend. People just have to know how to recognize them and then get help," explains John Walsh, host of *America's Most Wanted.* "Windows may be kept covered by towels or sheets. Women and girls may only be seen headed to church, yet men swarm in and out of the houses. The girls are moved through quickly, staying in one brothel for a week before switching locations."

No place in America is immune. Similar to its prevalence across the world, "there's no doubt that there is human trafficking in every state in the union," says Chief Assistant U.S. Attorney Douglas Molloy.

During a federal court hearing last year, Special Agent Angel Rascon-Rubio of the Bureau of Immigration and Customs Enforcement described *Phoenix,* Arizona as "the hub" of immigrant trafficking. He reported that "ninety percent of the transactions dealing with the sale of human cargo, those smuggled across the Arizona border, occur right here." Phoenix is ideal for hiding trafficking victims because it is close to the Mexican line, yet far enough away so there are no Border Patrol agents. Freeways servicing Phoenix provide nationwide access. And large Hispanic neighborhoods offer cover for traffickers and victims.

One of the largest trafficking organizations ever prosecuted in America was discovered in *Long Island*, a "major immigrant gateway" according to the U.S. Department of Justice. Sixty-nine Peruvian men, women, and children were lured into the country by promises of easy wealth only to find that they were forced to work sixteen hours a day in a small garment factory. Each person was told they owed traffickers $12,500 in transportation fees. Unable to pay down their debt while earning little or no money, they existed for four years in subhuman conditions inside three small houses with no outside contact allowed.

"We opened the door and looked at what these victims are subjected to, and you don't understand the depths" remembers Charlie Frost, a Collier County, *Florida*, Detective. "Brothels with young girls are hot spots in Collier and Lee Counties," he continues. "We were in one house and the oven was full of condoms. I mean full. They fell out when we opened the door. These girls are servicing thirty to forty men a day." In one house in Lee County, Florida, the brothel operators removed all the appliances from the kitchen to make room for more mattresses.

"We here in *Toledo* had no idea that this was going on," said Dave Bauer, an Assistant U.S. attorney in Toledo, Ohio. He explains that "the difficulty in finding traffickers who specialize in underage prostitution is that they run a mobile business."

Often, the girls are recruited in Toledo, but then quickly moved across the country, where "they would quite easily fly under our radar screens," Bauer says. "Toledo is one of the top cities in the country for teen prostitution," said Celia Williamson, a University of Toledo professor and author of the *Typology Of Street Prostitutes: Health and Well-Being*. Deborah Hodges, a Lucas County Juvenile Court, Ohio official, concurs, "One of the federal investigators told us that Toledo is the number one recruiting spot in the United States. It is mind-boggling."

"A major interstate highway that runs from California to Florida has become a magnet for human traffickers," states Attorney General Gonzales. The I-10 Highway, which passes directly through *New Orleans*, has been used heavily by those transporting children since Hurricane Katrina devastated the area. Jim Letten, a U.S. attorney based in New Orleans, says "the opportunity for exploitation in New Orleans is ripe.

Interstate 10, which skirts the Mexican border in Texas and runs through Louisiana, has traditionally been a pipeline for moving drugs. Now it's a route to move people," Letten explained. "New Orleans is a frontier town now."

In 2003, the U.S. Justice Department began operation *Innocence Lost,* a task force of federal agents dedicated to the investigation of child prostitution in 27 American cities. The project further illustrates how deeply this issue has infiltrated communities throughout the United States:

- In Chelsea, Massachusetts, Evelyn Diaz was charged with recruiting girls who were thirteen, fifteen and sixteen to work as prostitutes.
- Juan Rico Doss of Reno, Nevada was convicted of recruiting girls fourteen and sixteen to work as prostitutes in California. He told them to lie about their ages if they were arrested.
- In Detroit, four Ohio residents were charged with holding girls as prisoners and making them call their pimp *Daddy*.
- Indictments of sixteen people in Harrisburg, Pa., alleged that one twelve-year-old girl was forced to have sex to pay for her grandfather's crack cocaine.

"Child exploitation is the most hidden form of child abuse found in North America today. It is the nation's least recognized epidemic," states Richard Estes, author of the landmark study, *The Commercial Sexual Exploitation of Children in the U.S.* Why is it spreading so drastically? For the very same reasons it is growing so quickly around the world. "They do this because they do not have money. They do not have parents who can help them, or they just don't have parents at all," says Laurel Freeman, Director of SAGE – Standing Against Global Exploitation. "Just like the girls from Thailand, these girls do not have other options."

* * *

Wright Patterson Air Force Base is one of the largest and most important *military bases* in the United States. Located in Ohio, the base has a workforce of over 22,000 people and has over 70 military units. It is home to the second largest medical center in the Air Force and is the fifth largest employer in Ohio; the largest employer at a single location.

Wright Patterson is also destination for trafficking victims.

"U.S. military bases represent some of the greatest demand sites for sex services," reports an extensive study by the Florida Department of Children and Families. The report finds that "bases within the United States have created the market for an infrastructure of sex clubs, brothels and massage parlors similar to those found near military bases abroad."

Over the past few years, human rights organizations and the international media "have reported women being forced into prostitution for a clientele consisting of military service members, government contracts, and international peacekeepers," reports U.S. Representative Christopher Smith, Republican of New Jersey and author of the *Trafficking Victims Protection Act* of 2000. "Our need to examine this problem of human trafficking in the context of the Department of Defense arises from the fact that prostitution has historically coexisted alongside large populations of military forces." Smith began to focus on the U.S. military in 2002 upon learning of an investigation of U.S. troops in South Korea patronizing bars and other establishments where women from the Philippines and the former Soviet states were trafficked and forced to prostitute themselves.

In response, the Inspector General of the Defense Department investigated the situations in South Korea, Bosnia-Herzegovina and Kosovo. Their results identified "institutional weaknesses in our military's understanding and response to trafficking," Smith said. "Over the past half-dozen years, such evils have been documented in South Korea, southeastern Europe, the Congo, and Sudan. It is reprehensible that any person with a responsibility to protect civilians would participate in prostitution or otherwise encourage human trafficking."

* * *

"On every continent, countries are failing to live up to their obligation to protect the weak, and bring criminals to justice," stated John Miller, Director of the U.S. State Department's Office to Monitor and Combat Trafficking In Persons in testimony before the U.S. Congress. Miller is not alone is his conviction. "Every country can do more, including the United States. All countries must maintain and increase efforts to combat trafficking," said U.S. Secretary of State Condoleezza Rice in June of 2006.

State's 2006 version of the *Trafficking in Persons Report* listed twelve countries on Tier 3, those "whose governments do not fully comply with the minimum standards and are not making significant efforts to do so." Among them was *Saudi Arabia*, where, the report shows, "victims are subjected to physical and sexual abuse, non-payment of wages, confinement, and withholding of passports as a restriction on their movement," and where the "government did not adequately protect victims, sometimes arresting, punishing, and deporting them instead." This was the second year in a row Saudi Arabia had been given the Tier 3 status.

Fortunately, the Tier placement system implements sanctions for Tier 3 nations including, "withholding of funding for participation in educational and cultural exchange programs," and "U.S. opposition to assistance from international financial institutions such as the International Monetary Fund and the World Bank."

It is doubtful Saudi Arabia would be affected by any of these sanctions. In any event, the Bush Administration waived *any* sanctions against the Saudis despite their failure to take significant action against child trafficking. The consequence of the waiver is that children there will continue to be sexually abused, forced into domestic labor and made to ride in camel races.

"Actions like this send the wrong signal to nations, friend and foe alike, that turn a blind eye to this international horror. Ally or not, America cannot condone human trafficking by any nation, and that is what we seem to be doing," said Representative Smith. "I have said it time and time again, 'friends don't let friends commit human rights violations.'"

* * *

"For no matter who they are and what they are, they are our sisters and brothers, mothers and fathers, uncles and aunts. I know that day they weren't the only ones to cry, in fact it was the whole world who cried along with them. The time has come to rebuild our nations. To lift up our spirits and work together. We can't bring back the dead but we can make those who are left behind live again. Give them new hope."

Chimingalo, 17
Source: Save the Children

* * *

Fifteen

I am Teary

Discarded

* * *

Teary grew up in rural Cambodia. Her parents died when she was a child. In an effort to give her a better life, her sister forced her into marriage when she was thirteen. Three months later, during a visit to a fishing village, her husband rented a room in what Teary thought was a guest house. When she woke the next morning, her husband was gone. The owner of the house told her she had been sold by her husband for $300 and that she was actually in a brothel. For four years, Teary was used by five to seven men every day. In time, she contracted AIDS. The brothel owner discarded her when she became sick. She died of AIDS at the age of seventeen.

Source: U.S. State Department

* * *

The consequences of child trafficking are not global. They are much smaller, deeper and personal. While trafficking causes an endless wave of corruption, crime and destruction of all kinds, its most terrible consequences are thrust upon the individual children who are abused by it.

In many instances, though the number will never be known, the consequence is death. All the potential of a human life is lost to the depravity of the world. Everything a child could have been, the ideas, the love, the accomplishments . . . all gone.

The only possible solace is that the child is finally safe and at peace.

If the child survives, the damages are extensive. No child is prepared to cope with continuous, raw brutality. And, should they live, no child escapes unscathed. "These children are victimized twice; first by the handler who exploits them and secondly by the individual who solicits them," says Chris Swecker, Assistant Director of the FBI.

Whether the child is working in a field, a factory or on a mattress, the problem for child traffickers is that they must control their victims at all times, even when the child is not with them. Their solution is simple and very effective: *drugs*. Drug addiction will motivate a person, young and old, to do anything. If an addict has but one source for drugs, they are completely at the mercy of the supplier. The person supplying the drugs can literally turn the addict into a human robot, performing any act at will.

Moreover, drugs capture and finally enslave the last vestige of human freedom, *the mind*. No longer is the slave keeper bothered by the liberties available in free thought. The victim's mind is obliterated and focused only on the availability of the drugs. All thoughts are directed to what must be done in order to obtain the next fix. The worst situation imaginable for the victim is not getting it, so anything other than that is a better option. Nothing is too severe or humiliating or dangerous.

However, drugs alone cannot create a profitable girl for her owner. *Seasoning*, is a process where girls are raped, beaten and relentlessly subjected to physical and psychological abuse in order to break their will and make them completely submissive. The goal is to turn a child into a prostitute; to perform for customers and make the most money. This is accomplished most successfully by making her completely dependent on the person in power over her; by forcing her to believe that her self-esteem is based entirely on pleasing that one person.

To keep the victims isolated and unable to seek help, traffickers move them to unfamiliar surroundings, other countries or to places with completely different cultures and language. In every way possible, they are far away from home. Without contact with friends and family, victims lack any support systems. They have no one.

In many cases the exploitation of trafficking victims is progressive; a child trafficked into one form of labor may be sold, moved and abused in another. In Nepal, for example, girls recruited to work in carpet factories, hotels, and restaurants have been forced later into the sex industry in India. In the Philippines, and in many other countries, children who initially migrate or are recruited for the hotel and tourism industry, often end up trapped in brothels. Because the demand for children is constantly shifting, victims are often bought and sold many times over.

The sexual abuse of children causes physical, psychological and social harm that can last a lifetime. Children who have been abused may be rejected by their families and communities. They are highly vulnerable to drug addiction, physical violence, sexually transmitted infections including HIV, permanent damage to reproductive organs and early pregnancy.

The U.S. Department of Health & Human Services (HHS) determined several ongoing physical and mental symptoms suffered by victims of child trafficking:

- Sleeping and eating disorders
- Sexually transmitted diseases, HIV/AIDS, pelvic pain, rectal trauma and urinary difficulties from working in the sex industry
- Chronic back, hearing, cardiovascular or respiratory problems from endless days toiling in dangerous agriculture, sweatshop or construction conditions
- Fear and anxiety
- Depression, mood changes
- Guilt and shame
- Cultural shock from finding themselves in a strange country

- Posttraumatic Stress Disorder
- Increased rates of suicide
- Traumatic bonding with the trafficker

"Child victims of human trafficking face significant problems. Often physically and sexually abused, they have distinctive medical and psychological needs that must be addressed before advancing in the formative years of adulthood," reported Dr. Wade Horn, HHS Assistant Secretary for Children and Families.

Finally, and most fundamentally, child trafficking undermines the basic need of a child to grow up in a protective environment and the right to be free from sexual abuse and exploitation. It violates, as the United Nations declared, the "universal human right to life, liberty, and freedom from slavery in all its forms."

* * *

Sixteen

I am Rusa

We Demand It

* * *

Rusa is a fifteen-year-old orphan from Uzbekistan, was kidnapped in 2004. Rusa's aunt arranged her abduction to Dubai using a cousin's passport, because the aunt wanted to take Rusa's apartment. In Dubai, Rusa was sold to a slavery and prostitution gang and then worked in a brothel for two years. When she was no longer useable in prostitution, the traffickers sent her to a psychiatric center. An Uzbek human rights organization located her in Dubai and arranged to have her moved to a shelter. Then, they could begin working on taking her home. However, because her entrance into the United Arab Emirates was not legal (her traffickers had used a false passport), immigration service said she should serve a two-year prison sentence.

Source: U.S. State Department

* * *

Child trafficking has been addressed by governments, international organizations, and business networks. Since the late 1990s laws, regulations, and sanctions have been enacted, ratified and applauded. Yet, more children are becoming slaves every day.

In 2000 the United States Congress passed the *Trafficking Victims Protection Act* (TVPA), which provides immigration relief and social services to eligible victims of trafficking. This was a significant step in acknowledging the trafficking crisis in the U.S. and implementing laws to combat it. Before 2000, no comprehensive federal law existed to protect victims and prosecute traffickers. "We thought it was essential to target the criminals, slaveholders, who force these young children and women into unimaginable horrors. Contrary to common belief, human trafficking is not a criminal activity exclusive to foreign countries. It happens within our own borders, within our own communities," said U.S. Representative Christopher Smith, the author of the bill.

TVPA 2000 has provisions to help victims, specifies penalties for criminal activity, provides assistance to countries working to combat trafficking and institutes sanctions for countries refusing to cooperate.

More specifically, TVPA recognizes all forms of trafficking that place victims in forced labor, slavery, and involuntary servitude. It authorizes a temporary visa and permanent residence for trafficked persons who are willing to comply with "reasonable" requests for cooperation and who would "suffer extreme hardship involving unusual and severe harm upon removal." Work authorizations are available; funding is provided to service providers; foreign aid is authorized for prevention and assistance programs abroad; and federal personnel will be trained to identify and protect trafficked persons.

Congress updated and strengthened the law in 2003 and again in 2005. These improvements mandated additional efforts to combat trafficking in persons and approved appropriations for fiscal years 2006 and 2007 for $361 million to combat trafficking worldwide.

Additionally, the U.S. Department of State issues an annual *Trafficking in Persons Report* (TIP) which is mandated by Congress and cited throughout this book. Every year TIP provides an updated assessment of the actions individual foreign governments are taking to combat trafficking, including efforts, or lack thereof, to protect victims and punishing their exploiters.

With assistance from private charities and faith-based organizations, these assessments divide countries into three tiers. As explained in chapter 14, Tier 1 signifies that a country fully meets the requirements of the TVPA. Tier 2 countries do not meet the standards fully, but are working to improve. Tier 2 also includes a "watch list" of countries that are at risk of moving backward in their efforts and could face sanctions. Tier 3 countries face possible restrictions or sanctions in American aid or other measures if they do not take significant anti-slavery action immediately.

Other branches of the U.S. Federal Government are also taking significant action. For instance, the U.S. Department of Health and Human Services (HHS) has initiated a *Rescue and Restore Victims of Human Trafficking* campaign to identify and assist victims of human trafficking in the United States. HHS is seeking cooperation from faith-based organizations, health care providers, social service organizations, law enforcement agencies, and citizens in order to meet its objectives. To anyone who can be of service, the campaign provides education about trafficking, enabling those who interact with the public to know what to look for in order to identify trafficking victims. It also equips them with the necessary tools to help trafficking victims access benefits and services.

Outside the United States, The United Nations has also taken strides in addressing the issue of international child trafficking. The long-titled *Protocol to Prevent, Suppress and Punish Trafficking in Persons, especially Women and Children*, also referred to as the *Palermo Protocol*, supplementing the *UN Convention against Transnational Organized Crime,* was adopted in 2000. Despite the fact that many of its provisions are related to the criminalization of certain activities, border measures, security, control and validity of documents, the purpose of the protocol is:

- To prevent and combat trafficking in persons, paying particular attention to women and children;
- To protect and assist the victims of such trafficking, with full respect for their human rights; and

- To promote cooperation among States Parties in order to meet those objectives.

The Palermo Protocol also contains a very comprehensive legal definition of human trafficking under international law. In brief, it defines it as "the recruitment, transportation, transfer, harboring or receipt of persons by means of the threat or use of force or other forms of coercion, of abduction, of fraud, of deception, of the abuse of power or of a position of vulnerability or of the giving or receiving of payments or benefits to achieve the consent of a person having control over another person, for the purpose of exploitation. Exploitation shall include, as a minimum, the exploitation of the prostitution of others or other forms of sexual exploitation, forced labor or services, slavery or practices similar to slavery." The entire definition, far longer and more detailed than quoted here, covers virtually every aspect of trafficking with a strong emphasis on protecting the victim.

With a goal of cooperation among individual nations and law enforcement agencies, governments which accept, or ratify, the protocol are required to "prevent and combat trafficking in persons, protecting and assisting victims of trafficking and promoting cooperation among states in order to meet those objectives." Ratifying the Protocol obligates individual states to introduce national trafficking legislation within their own country.

Along with these provisions, The Palermo Protocol specifically addresses child trafficking by:

- facilitating the return and acceptance of children who have been victims of cross-border trafficking, with due regard to their safety;
- prohibiting the trafficking of children for purposes of commercial sexual exploitation of children, exploitative labor practices or the removal of body parts;
- suspending parental rights of parents, caregivers or any other persons who have parental rights in respect of a child should they be found to have trafficked a child;
- ensuring that definitions of trafficking reflect the need for special safeguards and care for children, including appropriate legal protection;

- ensuring that trafficked persons are not punished for any offences or activities related to their having been trafficked, such as prostitution and immigration violations;
- ensuring that victims of trafficking are protected from deportation or return where there are reasonable grounds to suspect that such return would represent a significant security risk to the trafficked person or their family;
- considering temporary or permanent residence in countries of transit or destination for trafficking victims in exchange for testimony against alleged traffickers, or on humanitarian and compassionate grounds;
- providing for proportional criminal penalties to be applied to persons found guilty of trafficking in aggravating circumstances, including offences involving trafficking in children or offences committed or involving complicity by state officials; and,
- providing for the confiscation of the instruments and proceeds of trafficking and related offences to be used for the benefit of trafficked persons.

Clearly, the Protocol recognizes that the complicated reality of child trafficking involves a multitude of circumstances.

The International Labor Organization (ILO) was founded in 1919 and is the only surviving major creation of the Treaty of Versailles which brought about the League of Nations. In 1946, the ILO became the first specialized agency of the United Nations. Since its inception, the ILO's mission has been to promote "social justice and internationally recognized human and labor rights."

In 1999, the ILO adopted the *Worst Forms of Child Labor Convention* in order to fight child trafficking, slavery and exploitation. By ratifying this Convention, a government commits itself to taking immediate action to prohibit and eliminate the "worst forms of child labor," which it defines as: "all forms of slavery or practices similar to slavery, such as the sale of a child; trafficking of children, meaning the recruitment of children to do work far away from home and from the care of their families, in circumstances within which they are exploited; debt bondage or any other form of bonded labor or serfdom; forced or compulsory labor, including forced or compulsory recruitment of children for use in armed conflict; commercial sexual exploitation of children, including the use, procuring or offering of a child for prostitution, or the production of pornography or for pornographic performances; use, procuring or offering of a child by others for illegal activities, also known as children used by adults in the commission of crime, including the trafficking or production of drugs."

Sex tourism has been specifically addressed by the *Code of Conduct for the Protection of Children from Sexual Exploitation in Travel and Tourism.* The Code was established by ECPAT, UNICEF and the World Tourism Organization in order to "prevent sexual exploitation of children at tourism destinations." It is aimed at making travel-related businesses responsible for protecting children against predators who use their services. "It is everyone's responsibility to protect children from commercial sexual exploitation," said Carol Smolenski, Director of ECPAT USA. "The code is a perfect example of how the travel industry can do its part in building a protective environment for children." Tour operators, travel agents, hotels, airlines, etc. which endorse the Code, commit themselves to:

- establishing a corporate ethical policy against commercial sexual exploitation of children;
- training their personnel in the country of origin and travel destinations;
- adding clauses to contracts with suppliers, stating a common repudiation of sexual exploitation of children;
- providing information relating to the prevention of child sex tourism to travelers through catalogues, brochures, in-flight films, ticket-slips, websites, etc;
- providing information to local "key persons" at destinations;
- report their annual progress and prevention activities.

"Every one of us is benefiting from slavery around the world," says Dr. Kevin Bales, Director of Free the Slaves. "We could eradicate slavery. The laws are already in force. The multinational and world trade organizations, the United Nations, they could end slavery. But they are not going to do it until and unless we demand it. "

* * *

Seventeen

I am Milah

They Are Among Us

* * *

Thomas is sitting on a small, dirty bed in a Cambodian brothel. His heart is racing. He is 49 years old, a retired Australian diplomat. He has a wife and two grown-up children back home. After a long, tense wait, a grinning teenaged boy opens the door and shoves two young girls into the room. He says one is seven years old. The other is nine. The younger one seems as nervous as Thomas. Her name is Milah. She is sweating and breathing heavily. As Thomas listens, the boy explains exactly what the girls will do for $60. Thomas sits back on the bed, a deliberately casual move, but it enables the top button on his shirt to point directly towards the girls' faces. Hidden within the button is a tiny video camera and microphone.

Source: BBC News

* * *

A child going into a dirty room to service another man does not care about conferences, reports, fact-finding missions, grants, research projects, or government agencies.

If it is not too late, she only cares about *staying alive and being safe.*

There are many government organizations working against trafficking. Across the globe, bureaucracies are focusing on it, studying it, holding meetings on it, giving speeches, having lunches, and generating statistics.

It isn't working. Whatever they are doing or not doing, children continue to be used, tortured, and disposed of for money.

Perhaps because the child trafficking is so hidden it becomes easy or convenient to let it remain a secret; a concept of a crime that merits only a concept of a response. Whatever the reason may be for the ineffectiveness of the world's governing bodies, the fact remains that child trafficking is the fastest growing crime in the world.

Did the firefighters and police conduct a lengthy study of the World Trade Center on 9/11? Did they hold meetings, roundtables, and conferences? No. They ran in and saved people who were in imminent danger. That is what you do when lives are at stake.

There are thousands of reports and studies all proclaiming what "must" be done to stop child trafficking. Several hundred of them were perused for this book. The common thread among all of them is the listing of recommendations that should be taken by governments, both the United States and others, to end child trafficking. Certainly, better law enforcement, more public awareness, reducing poverty, equal access to education and government pressure will all be effective over time, and if it can all be implemented everywhere in the world. However, while these many recommendations are brilliantly conceived and well intentioned by intelligent, caring people, not one makes the single suggestion to go and *rescue the children – now.*

The U.S. State Department's *Trafficking in Persons Report* states very clearly that "a victim-centered approach to trafficking requires us equally to address the 'three Rs' - *rescue, rehabilitation, and reintegration.*" Recently, Thomas, the man with the camera in his shirt, and his organization planned a raid on a brothel in Cambodia in order to rescue the young girls working there. Just after the raid they discovered the business was owned by a powerful local policeman. While it caused a lot of trouble with local authorities, the raid rescued three girls, the youngest was eleven. It also put two adults in jail, but not the policeman. Because of the scandal, Thomas says it now takes him many days, instead of hours, to get the police to respond to what they discover during the raids. While the work is dangerous, Thomas has a simple perspective on it. "Someone has to do this job. I guess it might as well be me."

Many have been exposed to the severity of the issue of child trafficking and child prostitution as it has gained heightened media attention including a special on *The Oprah Show*, the Lifetime mini-series *Human Trafficking*, NBC's *Dateline*, special reports from the *New York Times* and many others. One exceptional affect of this coverage has been to raise the risk of pedophiles, sex tourists and other exploiters of being caught. "The power of shame has stirred many to action and sparked unprecedented reforms. Defeating human trafficking is a great moral calling and we will never subjugate it to the narrow demands of the day," stated Condoleezza Rice, addressing the Independent Women's Forum in May of 2006.

"We need to go after these sick perverts, these sex tourists," states Guy Jacobson, producer of *The Virgin Harvest*, a film documentary exposing child sex trafficking in Cambodia. "Let's make them know they can't pay $50 to the police and walk away. We have to make the punishment for the customer so severe that no one will dare try to buy these kids." A former investment banker from Israel, Jacobson has determined that the best way to fight trafficking is to reduce the demand. "If the price is too high or too risky, the demand will dry up. If the demand dries up, the market will go away."

This may be one of the most effective ways to fight well funded, transnational crime gangs. "Poverty, abuse, discrimination, we know the root causes, who the vulnerable children are, where they come from. Clearly, to develop a tight, effective network that protects children, we must go to the source," said Maria Calivis, of UNICEF's Central and Eastern Europe division. "Time and again, opportunities to prevent or stop trafficking have been missed. To foil the predators, we must urgently become as organized and agile as they are."

* * *

"We need your dedication and energy and patience. The U.S. government can engage governments, we can seek to educate people around the world, but the fight to end modern slavery depends on the involvement of private organizations, regular citizens, individual diplomats, business people, and others. All of us must be committed to the new abolition movement of ending human trafficking."

Ambassador John R. Miller,
Former Director of the State Department's Office to
Monitor and Combat Trafficking in Persons

* * *

"When our grandchildren ask us where we were when the weak and the voiceless and the vulnerable of our era needed a leader of compassion and purpose and hope, I hope we can say that we showed up, and that we showed up on time," says Gary Haugen.

"Children don't vote." It is an old saying in politics that is supposed to explain why children do not merit fear and respect from elected leaders. The real reason children lose out in the political process is that adults fail to fight for children the way they fight for themselves. No, children don't vote, but neither do firearms, clean air, or whales. Adults protect their self-interests with money, lobbyists, and modern campaign strategies.

Children do not make political contributions, hire media specialists, nor form political action committees. Yet, every year in America, hundreds of powerful special interest groups and political candidates assemble teams of seasoned consultants, build up huge war chests, and conduct their own media and electoral campaigns. With vicious pursuit they fight for their objectives relentlessly.

Should we not be doing the same thing for children, *all children*? This is not a Red State-Blue State issue. It cannot be argued more from a liberal or conservative viewpoint. This is a non-partisan, non-political issue.

Concerned people everywhere can help victims by being aware of the problem, knowing the law and identifying potential victims in their daily life or when they are traveling. Anyone who has significant contact with the public in the United States can identify and assist victims of trafficking simply by being aware that *they are among us.*

* * *

Among the worst crimes committed against children, *inaction* is surely the most preventable. Every time you tell someone about what is happening to children around the world, each time you have the courage to speak the unspeakable, you are giving a voice to a child who suffers in the awful silence of slavery. There are many ways to help protect children from sexual exploitation and make a difference in someone's life. Below are a few ideas.

- Raise awareness about child trafficking. Write letters to legislators and publications. Organize lectures, conferences, and briefings with businesses, schools, religious institutions and community organizations.
- Be vigilant. Stay alert to all forms of human or child trafficking. Use your cell phone camera. Record addresses, license plates or activities. Keep in mind *forced labor* occurs almost everywhere.
- Report abuse. If you suspect abuse in the United States, contact the Trafficking in Persons and Work Exploitation Task Force at the U.S. Department of Justice: 888-428-7581. If you suspect abuse abroad, report it to *reliable* law enforcement, or to U.S. authorities.
- Contribute to effective organizations fighting child trafficking.
- Go to AhavaKids.org or call 888-584-6068. Ahava Kids is a human rights organization dedicated to rescuing and caring for young people victimized by the crime of child trafficking, enslavement and exploitation throughout the world. It is also the organization which benefits from the sale of this book. At AhavaKids.org you can:
    - stay informed;
    - sign up for the newsletter;

- help rescue and care for child victims through your donation;
- organize your own campaign.

- Regularly let your elected officials know that you oppose child trafficking and want protections for children everywhere in the world.
- Stay informed.
    - Find out if the U.S. government is enforcing sanctions against *all* countries that are not making significant efforts to eliminate trafficking. If they are not, ask them why through letters, emails, editorials, etc. A good place to start is at HumanRightsWatch.org.
    - Keep up to date on the quickly changing issues surrounding modern-day slavery in all its forms. As political situations shift, natural disasters strike, warfare erupts and transnational crime evolves, children face new dangers every day. The International Labor Organization is an excellent source of new information at ILO.org, as is the Protection Project of Johns Hopkins University at Protectionproject.org.
- Talk to your children about child trafficking and how to stay safe. Find out what to say and how to say it by contacting the experts, the National Center for Missing and Exploited Children at Missingkids.org.
- Be a Demanding Consumer. Currently, there is a U.S. law which prohibits the importation of products made with "forced or indentured child labor." However, with the massive amount of products imported into the United States, it is nearly impossible to enforce this law. You can help by knowing what you are buying.
    - Insist on Fair Trade products, especially for chocolate and coffee. This will ensure better lives by providing suppliers with enough money for health care, education for their children, and sustainable production methods. Go to Transfairusa.org for more information and to

Fairtradefederation.org for a list of Fair Trade retailers and wholesalers in your area.

- Look for the Rugmark label when purchasing wool rugs. This ensures that the manufacturer only employs skilled, adult artisans and that no child labor was used. Also, a portion of the price of your rug pays for the education of former child laborers. Rugmark provides an excellent model for ending slave labor and caring for its victims. Go to Rugmark.org for information and a list of retailers.
- Be selective when you travel by only using travel related services which adhere to the *Code of Conduct for the Protection of Children from Sexual Exploitation in Travel and Tourism*. You may be surprised by the names of major corporations in the travel industry which do not participate in this simple protocol. Go to Thecode.org to find out.

Whether in the United States or traveling abroad, if you suspect you may have come in contact with a victim of child trafficking, try to ask any of the following questions:

- Why did you come here?
- Who arranged your travel?
- How did you get here?
- Do you owe money for your trip?
- What did you expect when you came?
- What did you end up doing?
- Were you scared?
- Do you have any papers?
- Who has them?
- Are you in school?
- Are you working?
- What kind of work do you do?
- Are you paid?
- Do you owe money to your boss or someone else?
- Can you leave your job if you want?
- Where do you live?

- Who else lives there?
- Where do you sleep?
- Are you scared to leave?
- Has anybody threatened you to keep you from running away?
- Has anybody ever hurt you to make you stay?
- Has your family been threatened?

Again, if you suspect the child is a victim, contact *reliable* authorities. While traveling oversees, it is absolutely necessary to use caution in contacting law enforcement because, in many countries, corruption plays a central role in the ability of traffickers to operate. Consequently, reporting cases to the authorities in many countries should be done only after discussions with nongovernmental organizations knowledgeable on the trafficking situation in the country.

* * *

When a friend offered Lhamwah a well-paying job as a housekeeper in a nearby city, she decided to go. Lhamawah left her family in Yunnan Province, China and traveled with the friend and six other girls to Thailand. Arriving in Chaing Mai, Lhamwah was taken to a brothel where she was locked in a guarded room so she could not escape. She was forced to work as a prostitute even when she was sick. Though she tried to convince other girls trapped there to escape with her, they were fearful because they knew runaways were brutally abused if caught. After volunteers from the International Justice Mission traced Lhamwah's story from her home to Chaing Mai, they rescued her late one night during a daring raid on the brothel. They immediately took her to an aftercare home where she was given a safe place to live and heal. In time she began to receive an education and has begun a new life. Lhamwah has returned to live with her family.

Source: International Justice Mission

* * *

In the underdeveloped countries where child trafficking is prevalent, the best way to help young victims is often *raid* and *rescue.* Once children are located in a brothel, a factory or any other situation in which they are at risk, plans and personnel must be put into place quickly in order snatch the young people away before their abusers have a chance to realize what is happening or to react. It is not easy, safe or inexpensive. It is often dangerous and confusing. In every instance, however, one thing is certain; it is a matter of life and death.

As the locations of the children change often, intelligence must be acted upon with utmost speed and decisive action. Because corruption of law enforcement in these areas is commonplace, very few people have knowledge of the raids. They are conducted at night in most cases with escape routes and final destinations known well in advance.

Sometimes controversial, what cannot be questioned is the safety of the children being saved. "It is critical that advocates and other members of the community become more aware of child trafficking so that these victims can be identified and rescued and their traffickers can be brought to justice," notes Kay Buck, Executive Director of the Coalition to Abolish Slavery & Trafficking noted.

If the effective practice of *raid* and *rescue* is criticized it is often because those conducting them do not give priority to *relocation* and *rehabilitation.*

The need to rescue victims promptly is paramount, but rescue does not always end the suffering. Some areas lack adequate facilities to protect children and begin necessary healing. Children are sometimes jailed and further traumatized. They can even be deported without regard to their health or safety. If this happens, they may face retribution, even death, from the local traffickers back home. They might even be trafficked again, with more abuse added to their misery. On the other hand, if young victims are not deported after a successful raid and rescue, there may be retribution from the criminals in the areas they were held captive.

Relocation and *Rehabilitation* after they are rescued is absolutely necessary to the safety of child trafficking victims. Often overlooked, these require planning and substantial resources. For several reasons, it is often better for the child to be relocated to an area where he or she will not be recognized. Anonymity is often the safest method of protection when there are people in their home community and people where the raid took place who are motivated, for whatever reason, to continue destroying the child. The psychological and physical suffering by victims of sexual exploitation, involuntary servitude, bonded labor, or forced child soldiering present long-term challenges. Counseling, shelter, proper nutrition, clothing, medical attention, and education are all required to fully rehabilitate victims.

Certainly, a life saving practice, *raid, rescue, relocation* and *rehabilitation* do not require much; only courage, knowledge and a sacrificial devotion to children.

* * *

"In this netherworld, children are channeled into prostitution, begging and soliciting, labor on plantations, in mines, in markets, in factories and in domestic work. They are physically abused, their working conditions are dangerous, they don't go to school, they get little rest, they don't have health care, and they don't have the care and protection of their family. At a certain point, they may be regarded as expendable. They are usually scared, and with good reason. Their presence is often illegal; they have no papers, and usually no protectors. In combating the phenomenon of child trafficking, we must remember that its victims need protection."

Ann M. Veneman
Executive Director, UNICEF

* * *

Eighteen

I am . . .

The Unspeakable

* * *

"I could not stop her from bleeding. She looked at me and wanted me to do something for her, but I could do nothing. No one would help us. No one came. I held her body for such a long time. I didn't want to let her go. It was like she was asleep and I wanted her to wake up so we could leave that place. But she was not asleep. Before she died she tried to move her lips, to tell me something, but she could no longer speak."

Aakarshan, 14
Source: Anonymous rescue team member

"The trade in people is one of the most dangerous threats to civilization, alongside organized crime, terrorism, drug addiction and drug trafficking."

Russian President Vladimir Putin

"We must show new energy in fighting back an old evil. Nearly two centuries after the abolition of the transatlantic slave trade, and more than a century after slavery was officially ended in its last strongholds, the trade in human beings for any purpose must not be allowed to thrive in our time."

President George W. Bush

* * *

So often, *children are caught in the torrent of violence* that envelops the world. "No violence against children is justifiable; all violence against children is preventable," states an in-depth study on violence against children conducted by the United Nations in late 2006. The study confirms that "such violence exists in every country of the world, cutting across culture, class, education, income and ethnic origin. In every region, in contradiction to human rights obligations and children's developmental needs, violence against children is socially approved, and is frequently legal and State-authorized."

Child trafficking, often at the root of this violence, exists in a variety of forms and is influenced by a wide range of factors, most often beginning in poverty. "Those who traffic in human lives treat people as easily expendable and highly profitable. But behind each dollar sign is a human tragedy," explains former U.S. Attorney General John Ashcroft.

Child trafficking is not like other crimes. Illegal drugs and international drug crimes are conceptual to most of us. Gun smuggling and illegal arms are something that will probably never touch our lives. Trafficking is a "special kind of evil" that destroys the best and most innocent in all humanity. Its victims are defenseless, powerless and voiceless. It is unspeakable because it is unbearable to the human heart. Consequently, our silence has become the criminals' best weapon. While protecting ourselves from the repulsive and evil nature of this reality, we are doing a profound disservice to all children, especially those who need our attention the most.

"Whether we like it or not, we are now a global people," writes Kevin Bales. "We must ask ourselves: Are we willing to live in a world with slaves? If not, we are obligated to take responsibility for things that are connected to us, even when far away. If we can't choose to stop slavery, how can we say that we are free?"

The crimes against these children, while too horrible to face, must be dealt with. There can be no compromise in challenging this evil. The protection of children from violence is a matter of international urgency. Now that the scale and impact of this exploitation of children are becoming better known, there can be no excuse.

Governments and corporations must know that people are watching and that they demand an end to slavery. Children must be given the protection to which they have an unqualified right.

If we allow the exploitation of our children we are complicit in the death of our future and the perversion of our legacy.

It will take many voices to save those who have been silenced by child trafficking. It will take voices all over the world, speaking together, to fight the criminal organizations profiting from the torture of young people. It will take voices, loud voices, unified in the struggle to save children who cannot speak for themselves.

It will take many voices to speak the unspeakable.

It will take *our* voices.

* * *

"So often they are simply forgotten or shamelessly exploited as soldiers, laborers, or innocent victims in the trafficking of human beings. No effort should be spared to urge civil authorities and the international community to fight these abuses and to offer young children the legal protection they justly deserve."

Pope Benedict XVI

* * *

Contacts to report abuse and get more information regarding child trafficking.

Trafficking in Persons and Worker Exploitation Task Force
U.S. Department of Justice
Report abuse: 888-428-7581
usdoj.gov/crt/crim/tpwetf.htm

Office to Monitor and Combat Trafficking in Persons
U.S. Department of State
202-312-9639
state.gov/g/tip/rls/tiprpt/

Child Exploitation and Obscenity Section
Criminal Division
U.S. Department of Justice
202-514-5780
usdoj.gov/criminal/ceos

Violence Against Women Office
U.S. Department of Justice
202-307-6026
ojp.usdoj.gov/vawo

Office of Refugee Resettlement
U.S. Department of Health and Human Services
202-401-9246
acf.dhhs.gov/programs/orr

Administration for Children & Families
Anti-trafficking Campaign
U.S. Department of Health and Human Services
888-373-7888
acf.hhs.gov/trafficking/

Ahava Kids
P.O. Box 498
Old Saybrook, CT 06475-0498
USA
AhavaKids.org
Phone: 888-584-6068 (Toll Free in the U.S.)
860-318-0810
Fax: 860-577-8097

References

Human Trafficking and Modern Day Slavery in Ohio
Kathleen YS Davis
Coordinator Polaris Project Ohio
Wright State University

Predators Are Becoming More Sophisticated: Pornographers and Pedophiles Online
Kurt Eichenwald
Testimony given to the U.S. House of Representatives
on the sexual exploitation of children on the Internet
The New York Times
April 4, 2006

Testimony of Alice S. Fisher
Before the U.S. Congress Committee on Energy and Commerce Subcommittee on Oversight and Investigations Concerning Sexual Exploitation of Children over the Internet: What Parents, Kids and Congress Need to Know About Child Predators
May 3, 2006

The United States *Trafficking and Violence Protection Act* of 2000

With Child Sex Sites on the Run, Nearly Nude Photos Hit the Web
Kurt Eichenwald
The New York Times
August 20, 2006

Let's Fight This Terrible Crime Against Our Children
Andrew Vachss
Parade, February 19, 2006

Testimony of Alice S. Fisher, Assistant Attorney General, Criminal Division, United States Department of Justice before the Committee on Commerce, Science, and Transportation, United States Senate Concerning "Online Child Pornography"
September 19, 2006

Human Trafficking's Profits Spur Horrors
Dennis Wagner
The Arizona Republic
Jul. 23, 2006

Heroic Young Girl Tells of Her Child Porn Ordeal
ABC News, Primetime
Aired December 1, 2005

Methods and Motives: Exploring Links between Transnational Organized Crime and International Terrorism
Dr. Louise I. Shelley, Principal Investigator
Transnational Crime and Corruption Center
American University
Washington, DC
National Institute of Justice Report, July 2005

Broken Bodies – Broken Dreams: Violence Against Women Exposed
Integrated Regional Information Networks (IRIN)
United Nations Office for the Coordination of Humanitarian Affairs
August, 2006

Trafficking in Human Beings: The Slavery that Surrounds Us
Ann Jordan
Initiative Against Trafficking in Persons

Nations Build Alliances to Stop Organized Crime
Pino Arlacchi
United Nations Office for Drug Control and Crime Prevention

Human Trafficking as 21st Century Slavery
Dr. Carol Allais
International Organization for Migration
University of South Africa

Child Slavery On African Cocoa Farms
Nooshin Shabani
UNICEF Global Exchange

The End of Child Labour: Within Reach. Global Report
International Labor Organization, 2006

AFRICA: The Dark Side of Chocolate
CorpWatch
Kate McMahon
October 28th, 2005

Child Labor Abuse Increases
William C. Mann
The Washington Post
September 6, 2006

Borderline Slavery: Child Trafficking in Togo
Jonathan Cohen
Human Rights Watch
April, 2003

The Relationship Between Child Domestic Servitude and the Sexual Exploitation of Children
United Nations Commission on Human Rights
Sub-Commission on the Promotion and Protection of Human Rights
Working Group on Contemporary Forms of Slavery
27th Session

Global Trends in Child Labour 2000–2004
International Programme on the Elimination of Child Labour
Statistical Information and Monitoring Programme on Child Labour (SIMPOC)
International Labour Office
2006

Inside the Home, Outside the Law: Abuse of Child Domestic Workers in Morocco
Clarisa Bencomo
Human Rights Watch
December, 2005

Low-Wage Economy Destroys The American Dream
Joseph T. Hansen
United Food and Commercial Workers
October, 2004

The Hidden Face of Globalization
Produced by Crowing Rooster Arts
and The National Labor Committee
November, 2003

Child Labor Here and Abroad
Linda F. Golodner
National Consumers League
January 21, 1998

Personal Perspective - Child Labor Beneath Our Feet
Louis Freedberg
San Francisco Chronicle
March 18, 2006

Swept Under the Rug: Abuses Against Domestic Workers Around the World
Judith Sunderland
Human Rights Watch
July, 2006

France to Tackle Romanian Prostitution and Begging Networks
Martine Veron
Agence France Presse
August 29, 2002

Human Rights Report on Trafficking in Persons, Especially Women and Children: A Country-by-Country Report on a Contemporary Form of Slavery: France
The Protection Project
July, 2006

Boys Forced to be Camel Jockeys in UAE
Jim Popkin
NBC News
September 12, 2006

Child Camel Jockeys in the Gulf States
Child Workers in Asia
CWA Newsletter, Vol. 13 , no. 2-3
April – October, 1997

A Global Horror: Young Women Forced into Marriage
Glamour
April 9, 2006

Early Marriage: Child Spouses
Stephen H. Umemoto
United Nations
March, 2001

Child Marriage in Developing Countries
Dr. Geeta Rao Gupta
Remarks given to the U.S. Department of State
September 14, 2005

Poverty, Illiteracy, and Child Marriage: A U.S. Response
Charlotte M. Ponticelli
Remarks given to the U.S. Department of State
September 14, 2005

Trafficking in Persons: USAID's Response
U.S. Agency for International Development
Office of Women in Development
2004

Opening a Window on North Korea's Horrors
Doug Struck
Washington Post Foreign Service
October 4, 2003

Betrayal
Bill Gertz
Regnery Publishing, Inc.
2001

A Situational Analysis of Child Sex Tourism in India
Agra, Delhi, Jaipur
ECPAT
December, 2003

Child Prostitution in India
Joseph Gathia
Concept Publishing Company, New Delhi
1999

Trafficking in Women and Children in India
Action Research on Trafficking in Women and Children in India
United Nations Development Fund for Women
National Human Rights Commission
Institute of Social Sciences
2003

Organised Crime and Human Trafficking
Thahn-Dam Truong
Institute of Social Studies
2001

Transplantation, Bodily Integrity, and the International Traffic in Organs
Nancy Scheper-Hughes
The Bellagio Task Force
1997

Laos PDR
International Program on the Elimination of Child Labor Mekong Subregional Project to Combat Trafficking in Women and Children
September 2004

Lack of jobs in Moldova leaves children without parental care
Vladimir Lozinski
UNICEF
October 18, 2006

Trafficking of children for labor and sexual exploitation in Moldova: results of a rapid assessment survey
Institute for Public Policy, Moldova Republic
2004

Trafficking in Human Beings: Global Patterns
Antonio Maria Costa
United Nations Office on Drugs and Crime
April 2006

Children at risk in Europe's modern slave trade
Associated Press
Sep 24, 2006

Ghosts Haunt Forgotten Former Sudan Slave
August 21, 2006
Opheera McDoom
Reuters

Traffickers Target Haitian Children
BBC News
August 11, 2002

A Life in the Day: Somaly Mam
John Follain
The Sunday Times Magazine
December 4, 2005

Global Diary: Cambodia
Mariane Pearl
Glamour
September, 2006

Briefing on Trafficking in Children
Ann M. Veneman
Executive Director, UNICEF
Testimony before the U.S. Congressional Human Rights Caucus
June 6, 2002

Work among Trafficked Women in Thailand
Sister Supaporn Chotiphol, R.G.S.
Pontifical Council for the Pastoral Care of Migrants and Itinerant People
December, 2003

Letting Them Fail: Government Neglect and the Right to Education for Children Affected by AIDS
Human Rights Watch
October 11, 2005

Interview with Dom Nutt
Christian Aid
March 3, 2006

Lesotho – The Mountain Kingdom
Transformation Resource Centre
October, 2006

A Nation of Orphans
Mail & Guardian – Johannesburg
AIDS Education Global Information System
August 21, 2003

Sex tourism: Lessons learned in Costa Rica
Philip Wright
BBC News
June 18, 2004

Justice Department, FBI, Announce Arrests Targeting Child Prostitution Rings in Pennsylvania, New Jersey, and Michigan
U.S. Department of Justice Press Release
December 16, 2005

Spotting signs key in trafficking probes
Kristen Zambo
Naples News
August 29, 2006

Gonzales Cites I-10 in Human Trafficking
Becky Gohrer
Associated Press
October 4, 2006

The Commercial Sexual Exploitation of Children in U.S., Canada and Mexico
Richard J. Estes
University of Pennsylvania School of Social Work Center for the Study of Youth Policy
2002

Who Is There to Help Us?
How the System Fails Sexually Exploited Girls in the United States
Sara Ann Friedman
ECPAT USA
2005

Florida Responds to Human Trafficking
Florida Department of Children and Families
Office of Refugee Services
December, 2005

Smith Relentless in Fight Against Trafficking
U.S. Representative Christopher Smith
Press Release
June 21, 2006

Child Trafficking and What to do About it
Mike Dottridge
International Federation Terre des Hommes
May, 2004

Testimony of Gary Haugen
Before U.S. House of Representatives
September 14, 1999

International Trafficking in Women to the United States: A Contemporary Manifestation of Slavery and Organized Crime
Central Intelligence Agency
November, 1999

Look Beneath The Surface
U.S. Department of Health & Human Services
Fact Sheet
August, 2006

Trapping Cambodia's sex tourists
Andrew Harding
BBC News
June 11, 2005

Disposable People: New Slavery in the Global Economy
Kevin Bales
University of California Press
September, 1999

Coming in April, 2007

Fatal Flaw

The Continued Failure of American Churches in the Post 9/11 World

By Raymond Bechard

The Sunday after September 11, 2001, houses of worship across the United States were filled to capacity. Crowded into the pews were people who wouldn't ordinarily be there. *This* was no ordinary Sunday. For the first time in two generations, Americans urgently looked to religion for something that would ease their fear and pain.

They didn't find it.

One month later the pews were empty again.

"Fight like a man."
Thomas Kempis
The Imitation of Christ

"Please, no explanations inside the church."
From a sign posted on a Christian Church in Jerusalem

* * *

It was a beautiful, sunny Sunday morning in New England. Late summer is especially kind to the coastline of Connecticut. The air isn't heavy anymore. It's bright and clear and fresh. It can dazzle your soul – if you're outside.

I wasn't. I had work to do.

Sitting on an old chair on the altar of an old church, I waited patiently for my turn to speak to the pleasant congregation before me. As they stared at the minister and then at the choir and then back at the minister, they surely wondered who I was. But, they knew the drill. After all, not everyone got to sit up there looking back at the people in the church. I *must* be *somebody* and they would find out sooner or later. Little did they know this is the only way I feel comfortable in a church, *so my back isn't to the door.*

If you have ever sat on a stage in front of an audience, you know it takes a little getting used to. The entire crowd is facing you, and you are the only one facing them. You are incredibly outnumbered. Suddenly, you become very aware of everything. Your eyes are more attentive, your back is straighter, and if you are in church, you pretend to sing more clearly. Every time I do this it feels like I am in church for the first time. Maybe that's why I always know where the door is . . . and the quickest path to it.

Yet, here I was, waiting my turn to speak. Waiting for everyone to look at me, expecting me to say something *astounding.* The way things turned out this particular Sunday, they were about to get their wish.

It was about 45 minutes into the 8:00 o'clock morning worship service and things were going well so far. We were in the final stages of a very successful capital campaign for this exquisite colonial Church in Mystic, Connecticut. As an advisor to churches and ministries across

America, I am often asked to address the people with a Sunday morning pep talk. Motivating those last few people to make their pledge as a financial campaign nears completion is much more effective if the rest of the program has been conducted properly. And this one had.

However, I had a challenge ahead of me. Sitting in that old church chair, in that old New England church, I realized I had to address an old church problem. In front of me were a few hundred people in a town of several thousand who came to church on Sunday for no particular reason other than habit, tradition and socialization. Most were there because it was a very pleasant and proper thing to do on a nice Sunday morning. But, that mindset and the culture that propagated it were clearly not enough to keep this church alive and growing. For this place to become and remain a vibrant, influential element of this community, the way it had been for the first one hundred years of its history, the people were going to have to face the challenges ahead with a different attitude.

If they didn't, then this church, like thousands of others across America, was in trouble.

Gazing out at the people, half listening to the announcement about the upcoming bake sale, I understood the pressure on me and the importance of the little talk I was about to give. The excellent people on the campaign committee were very clear about the points they wanted me to make. But, it was up to me as to how I would make the message powerful enough to stick. As I assessed the congregation that morning I knew it wasn't going to be easy. There was a fundamental problem: the people were here in church for their own reasons, but we were asking them to give real money for reasons totally irrelevant to them.

The stakes were indeed high. This church had to move forward or it would wither on the vine. They could not stand still. Keeping the status quo wasn't an option. The population of the church was aging and there would be no one left in a few years. If they didn't start actively investing in the church right now, then its future would never be as bright as the magnificent skies outside.

I said a quick prayer - *yes, it had come to that* - for God to guide me in my words.

"And now, I would like to introduce you to someone who has been working with our campaign committee for several months behind the scenes." That was me. My turn at bat.

I stood up and walked forward. I had made some quick notes on the church's Sunday bulletin. I held it in my hand. When I reached the podium I tucked the bulletin next to the Bible that was open in front of me. The microphone waited for me to speak into it. I tried to remember what I had scribbled on the paper. Not a word came to me. Nothing. "*Oh God,*" I prayed silently, "*please make this your message.*" This prayer, while extremely helpful and effective, is also the last bastion of a desperate public speaker.

Then, something occurred to me. I thought about what my friend Andre had said to me a few years ago. I was planning a January trip to Moscow for a ministry I was working with at the time. I finally reached him on the phone at his apartment near Red Square. "Hey, Andre, what kind of clothes should I wear in the winter in Russia? I don't want to be cold," I asked him. "No," he said. "You are not cold in Russia in the winter. You are either warm or dead."

I knew exactly what he meant. Sometimes you can't afford to be cold, to stay in one place or be stagnant. You either prepare for the cold, or you are dead from it. If you are not ready, if you are caught unprepared, then it's already too late. The cold will kill you.

You are either warm or dead.

"My father," I began, "was a gunner in a B-29 in the Pacific during World War II."

This is definitely not in my notes.

"My stepfather was B-24 pilot. My Pastor, a radio man in a B-17."

I have no clue where this is going.

"My mother worked for the USO and in a factory in Hartford, making engine parts for airplanes."

The only thing I knew after I said all this – because I certainly had *no idea* what I was going to say next – was that all the *older* people in the congregation were not only paying attention, they were smiling.

Okay, maybe I'm on to something here.

"I'm telling you this because I want to speak to those of you who are of their generation. I'm not excluding the rest of you. You can listen along. But, there is something I have to say especially to those of you who came of age when Franklin Roosevelt was President. You were raised in the Great Depression. It has always been hard for me to even comprehend the scope of that era. It was such a different world then. Perhaps it's always hard for younger generations to find a point of reference or commonality with days past. It was difficult beyond anything that younger generations have ever known. That's why I am always amazed at the fondness I hear in your voices when you talk about those days. Because every time you tell the stories, you speak with such longing. Yet, all those stories begin with the same phrase, 'We had nothing.'

"I don't know what it is to have nothing. Or to live in a nation of people who *all* have nothing. You were children, of course, but you were growing up in smaller communities that looked after one another and supported each other. You knew your neighbors, they knew you. You went to church on Sundays and so did everyone else. You had each other to turn to in times of trouble. You were not isolated or alone, but a part of a great struggle to survive and make it through each day.

"Then, sixty years ago, began the greatest open conflict in the history of the world. You took the character and courage the Depression had given you and fought against the most powerful armies on earth. Now, please understand that not too many things really hold me in awe. But what you did during those years, well, I can't even begin to express my amazement. It's not an overstatement to say that you, all of you, men and women, saved the world.

"Then, you came home. And you built everything. It was your generation that produced this modern nation. You started the businesses, invented the machines, built the roads, bridges, factories, and schools. Growing up, we just thought they had always been there. What did we know? But, it was you. All along, it was all of you.

"It was you who had been molded as children during the Depression, put to the test as young people during World War II, and had the character to build a great nation as adults.

"And now, I stand before you to tell you that I'm scared."

I paused here because I was getting choked up. My stepfather had died two years earlier and I was thinking of him. He was the pilot I mentioned a few moments ago and everything I was saying now, was about him. His face was right in front of me.

"I'm scared, because we're losing you. And God help us all when you're gone.

"You have watched how the world has changed. You have seen the worst and best of humanity. You have seen your grandchildren growing up in prosperity and abundance. You have seen the ease at which we go about our lives.

"And you know it can't last forever.

"You know their day will come, because you're old and wise enough to know that it always comes. You know a time is coming that will test their character. You know someday they will find themselves in a crisis, and they will need a place they can turn to.

"Will they come to the church when they are in peril? Will they look for answers here? And if they do, will they find what they are looking for?

"I want to ask you something, you of that great generation. Do you think we're ready? Do you think we have what it takes to face the dangers that lay ahead? You know they're coming. You know that day is coming when the people will show up at the door of this church, looking for something. Hope. Safety. Shelter.

"Are we ready for that day when your grandchildren realize the world is not as safe and secure as they've been lead to believe?

"And is the church prepared to face the consequences if we're not ready for that day? What if they find us still fighting with each other, still deciding whether or not get new hymnals, still gossiping, and still ignoring them? What if we are arguing politics instead of agreeing that we are here to help people? What if we are all too busy clinging to traditions rather than faith?

"What then?

"I just want to suggest that maybe we should prepare for that day. Maybe we should focus on what is really important. Put ourselves aside and serve the Lord and His people. He's made it pretty clear what we should do. He gave us His incredible Son as an example.

"So what are we waiting for?

"Should we wait for that one Sunday when trouble comes and people we have never seen before are desperately looking answers? Do we start then?

"I am only saying that, as a church, we must be absolutely ready and totally prepared when the masses come through these doors."

I had said enough. I thanked them for their dedication and for allowing me to speak. Before finishing, I made a quick glance at my scribbled notes on the bulletin in front of me to make sure I didn't miss anything. The only thing I remember seeing is the date on the cover, "September 9, 2001."

One week later, that Sunday came. And we weren't ready.

* * *

About the Author

Raymond Bechard is Founder and Director of Ahava Kids, an international Human Rights organization which rescues young people from the crime of child trafficking, enslavement and exploitation throughout the world. Raymond lives on the shoreline in Connecticut.